winter
trails ™

COLORADO

Help Us Keep This Guide Up to Date

Every effort has been made by the authors and editors to make this guide as accurate and useful as possible. However, many things can change after a guide is published—new products and information become available, regulations change, techniques evolve, etc.

We would love to hear from you concerning your experiences with this guide and how you feel it could be improved and be kept up to date. While we may not be able to respond to all comments and suggestions, we'll take them to heart and we'll make certain to share them with the authors. Please send your comments and suggestions to the following address:

The Globe Pequot Press
Reader Response/Editorial Department
P.O. Box 480
Guilford, CT 06437

Or you may e-mail us at:
editorial@globe-pequot.com

Thanks for your input, and happy travels!

*A*FALCONGUIDE®

WINTER TRAILS™ SERIES

winter trails™

COLORADO

The Best Cross-Country Ski
& Snowshoe Trails

Second Edition

by

TARI & ANDY LIGHTBODY

FALCON®

GUILFORD, CONNECTICUT
HELENA, MONTANA

AN IMPRINT OF THE GLOBE PEQUOT PRESS

A FALCON GUIDE®

Photographs: pp. xiv, 60, 67, 71, 79, 104, 106, John W. Singleton; p. xv, Tari and Andy Lightbody; pp. xvi, xxiii, 15, 32, David Singleton; pp. xxiv, 134, 147, Rochelle Bernstein; pp. 1, 158, Tom Stillo, courtesy of Crested Butte Mountain Resort; pp. 4, 5, courtesy of Never Summer Nordic, Inc.; pp. 6, 43, 118, 119, 124, courtesy USDA Forest Service; p. 50, Jack Affleck / Keystone Resort; p. 90, courtesy of Summit Huts Association; p. 96, Louise Singleton; p. 100, Todd Powell, courtesy Summit Huts Association; p. 115, Greater Leadville Area Chamber of Commerce; p. 130, Rob Gracie, courtesy of Aspen Skiing Company; p. 170, Roy Kasting, courtesy of O_2 Productions, www.western-light.com

Project Editor: David Singleton
Text design: Nancy Freeborn
Trail maps created by Equator Graphics © The Globe Pequot Press
State map: Lisa Reneson

ISSN 1546-332X
ISBN 0–7627–2522–2

Manufactured in the United States of America
Second Edition/Second Printing

Contents

Winter Trails Colorado

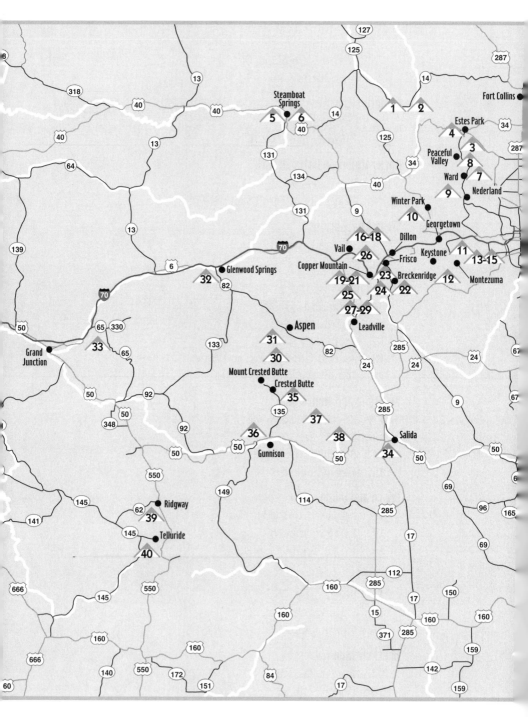

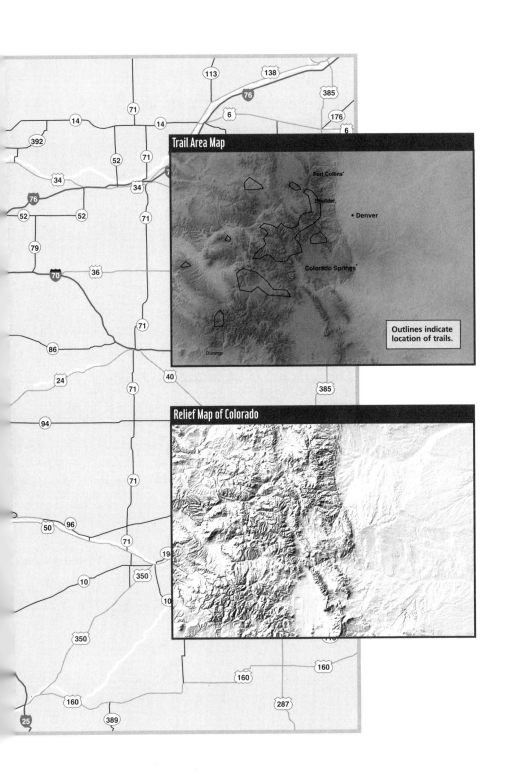

Trail Area Map

Fort Collins

Boulder

• Denver

Colorado Springs

Durango

Outlines indicate location of trails.

Relief Map of Colorado

Dedication

This book is dedicated to our four great children who often went "in tow" along with us to visit the many areas and trails, and to Ray and Betty Lightbody for helping watch "The Rugrats" when it required long writing sessions.

To the kids:

Daniel "where's the double black diamond" Lightbody

Jeffrey "where's the snowboard trail" Lightbody

Matthew "uh, I have just one question to ask you," Lightbody

Jennifer "how do I look?" Lightbody

To the Grandparents:

Betty "I'm in charge here" Lightbody

Ray "It's okay with me, but go ask your Grandmother" Lightbody

To Everyone—Thank You!!

Acknowledgments

Winter Trails Colorado could not have been compiled and written without a lot of input, direction, suggestions, and assistance from those individuals, organizations, associations, state and federal agencies, and ski resorts that have worked and continue to work so hard to make Colorado the premier state for winter outdoor recreation.

Our special thanks to the following: Jenifer Blomquist of 10th Mountain Division Hut Association; Tom Ela of Grand Mesa Nordic Council; Sunlight Mountain Resort; Lynn Thompson of Never Summer Nordic, Inc.; Leslie McFadden, Kevin Cannon, John Anarella, Ed Patalik, Mary Beth Higgins, Paul Cruz, Ralph Bradt, Ted Hinrichs, Jimmy Gaudry, Bill Jackson, Tim Lamb, Erik Martin, and Jon Morrissey of the USDA Forest Service for being helpful and patient through a tough fire season; Joe Evans of Rocky Mountain National Park; Melissa Kuwahara and Mike Zobbe of Summit Huts Association; Hawk Greenway of Alfred Braun Hut Association; Murray Cunningham of Friends Hut Association; Joe Ryan of San Juan Hut System; Jed Frame and Mary Frame of Elkton Cabins; and Carrie Hudson of Monarch Ski and Snowboard Resort.

Introduction

In our writing careers, which between the two of us total close to 45 years, *Winter Trails Colorado* has to rate as one of the most challenging books we've ever written. The problem lies in the fact that Colorado has so many great cross-country ski and snowshoe trails for the backcountry explorer that trying to sort through the thousands of trails and backcountry areas was a most daunting task. Unlike other states, where the cross-country ski and snowshoe trails are predominantly found to be perfectly groomed and almost always in and around ski areas and their companion nordic centers, the trails in Colorado often offer the outdoorsperson true backcountry adventures and experiences.

Many times restaurants, overnight accommodations, and even convenience stores are located miles away from the trails. And although the trails presented here range from the novice all the way through to advanced levels, the underlying theme and caution is *if you backcountry ski or snowshoe anywhere in the Rocky Mountains, you must be self-sufficient and plan to be self-reliant.*

Trail Selections and Ratings

Trails that are highlighted in this book are some of the best that you'll find anywhere in the state of Colorado. They're also some of the best that you'll find anywhere in the country! They are not, however, always the most popular or famous trails for cross-country skiing or backcountry snowshoeing. Although many of the trails are well traversed, the routes we present represent a complete spectrum and variety of trails, for all levels of skiing and snowshoeing abilities. We selected some of the trails simply because they are not the most popular—translating to a better quality backcountry experience: fewer crowds, unspoiled scenery, and plenty of solitude.

Many of the trails profiled in *Winter Trails Colorado* are found in areas where there are countless other trails that wind, intersect, and meet up with the profiled route. Nordic centers, ski areas, and locals in all of these areas are likely to have "their" favorite trails as well. Visiting the area where a trail is profiled will likely lead you to other "favorites" of your own. The nice thing about Colorado is that there are many great trails for just about every skiing and snowshoeing ability.

Early season skiing above Janet's Cabin.

Fifteen years ago, snowshoeing as a recreational sport was in its infancy. Downhill and cross-country skiing in Colorado were the rage with just about everyone. Today, skiers and snowshoers are found in the backcountry in unprecedented numbers. Everyone from the beginner, looking for a casual wilderness stroll, to the expert, craving a real aerobic workout, are all on the trails!

As you read through *Winter Trails Colorado,* pay close attention to how each of the trails is classified: novice, intermediate, or advanced. The **novice trails** are designed to be relatively easy, for those who are first-timers or who have limited trail experience. These trails are the ones that are relatively short in duration and usually can be accomplished in a half day or less. They are also ones that are well marked, have relatively flat terrain, and include mild ascents and descents.

The **intermediate trails** are suited to those who have some backcountry trail experience and are comfortable with their abilities to ski or snowshoe both on and off the beaten path. The trails are longer and can take four hours to a full day to accomplish. These trails are designed for skiers and snowshoers who have good map-reading skills, are not intimidated by having to break their own trail, and are seeking more challenging terrain in terms of ascents and descents.

The **advanced trails** are just that! They are designed for skiers and showshoers with lots of backcountry experience and abilities. These trails are long and most will take anywhere from five hours to several

A lesson can help you enjoy skiing more.

days to complete. They are designed for those with appropriate equipment and excellent backcountry winter survival skills. These trails may have steep climbs and descents.

Whatever your ability, taking a lesson can help you become better. Whether it is learning the basics of the kick-and-glide for the first time or getting advice on your telemark turn in powder, taking a lesson will help you feel more comfortable and confident when you are on the trail in the backcountry. Most nordic centers offer lessons in a variety of skills, and it is okay to get some help.

Our best advice is to ski or snowshoe at your own personal ability level. Don't try to be a hero and think you can just go for it. That's a dangerous decision that will get you into trouble in a hurry! Select trails that are within your skill level. It's always pleasant to select a trail that leaves you fulfilled and with great memories. It's a nightmare to discover too late that you have overestimated your abilities.

One more thing to consider: The mileages for all of the trails represent the round trip distance unless one way is specified.

Be careful to acclimate to Colorado's high altitude.

Altitude

Cross-country skiing and snowshoeing in the backcountry require a considerable amount of physical exertion. If you're not accustomed to the high-altitude conditions found in the state, you're liable to put your health at risk and jeopardize your high mountain adventure or expedition.

If you're not already a Colorado resident, and you drive or fly to Colorado, you're going to need a little time to adjust to the thin Rocky Mountain air. Keep in mind, that even before you head up into the mountains, you're already about 1 mile above sea level. To enjoy all of the trails in *Winter Trails Colorado* means that you will be exercising at even higher elevations.

Unless you're already used to the high-altitude climbing, skiing, and trekking that's required to enjoy these trails, you may want to spend the day of your arrival relaxing and adjusting to the new conditions. There's a lot less oxygen to breathe in the mountains. As we like to tell visitors to the area, "It's beautiful up here, but bring your own air!" Jumping from at or near sea level to Colorado can easily bring on a case of altitude sickness.

The chronic symptoms of altitude sickness include headache, nausea, tiredness, and shortness of breath. Doctors at the Denver Health Medical Center say that 60 percent of people will suffer from a mild to severe case of altitude sickness by traveling at or above 8,000 feet. A variety of supposed cures—such as taking aspirin, vitamins, and various herbs—are always being touted, but results vary widely from person to person. The best bet is to spend the first day taking it easy. Get plenty of rest, drink plenty of liquids, eat well, avoid alcohol and coffee, and keep your physical exertion to a comfortable level.

If you start to suffer from altitude sickness, you're going to have to slow down or you're going to be miserable. Remember food, rest, and plenty of liquids are about the only way to combat the effects of altitude sickness, short of coming down to a lower elevation.

Equipment and Survival Gear

Equipment for cross-country skiing and snowshoeing has changed radically over the past few years. It's not that the older equipment isn't good, but the new high-tech equipment being introduced is often lighter, stronger, and more versatile than what was offered even five years ago.

Snowshoes almost always have built-in grips on the bottom of the shoes for climbing and traction. Cross-country skis for Colorado are going to require what are called *climbing skins;* they're traction devices that are either glued or strapped onto your skis' bottom surfaces to keep you from sliding backward while climbing. Without them—on either waxless or waxable skis—you're going to find that the climbs are much more difficult, if not impossible. Although there are a lot of different types of skis that work well in the backcountry, the best are sturdy skis with metal edges. Track equipment is often too flimsy and hard to control in backcounty situations where the track may be uneven or not groomed. Sturdy boots, similar to hiking boots, will help stabilize your ankles and enhance your control and sense of security.

Because just about all the trails are loaded with lots of up and down climbing or gliding, a good set of ski or snowshoe poles is another must. For snowshoeing, regular commercial fixed-length downhill poles will suffice. But for cross-country skiing use poles that are longer and made for the purpose. These tend to be lighter, and the top of the handle should come to between your armpit and the top of your shoulder. This will give you the length to push off with force even while going uphill. Regular length alpine poles are too short, and you'll find yourself struggling when you climb. The best and most practical poles for backcountry adventures are those that adjust in length and convert to avalanche probe poles. These can be used for locating avalanche victims. We hope you'll never need them to fill this function, but it's always best to be prepared. You can also shorten these kind for skiing down slopes.

If you're new to the world of cross-country skiing and snowshoeing, it's probably best to rent your equipment the first few times you go out. This way you can sample a variety of makes, models, and styles from a host of different makers and manufacturers. Once you decide what you like and what fits your style, then it's time to make a purchase. Ski shops, resorts, and nordic centers throughout the state rent equipment for everything from a half day to a week or more. Some even will work a package deal on rental equipment for the entire season.

Selecting the right clothing for your backcountry adventures is of paramount importance. As with the ski and snowshoe industries, the revolution in clothing for the winter enthusiast has resulted in a host of lighter weight, warmer, water-resistant, and breathable miracle fabrics. Volumes could be written on the subject of clothing only. Suffice it to say that in Colorado, the weather is predictably unpredictable. You can literally get up in the morning with a bright blue sky and moderate temperatures only to get out on a backcountry trail and encounter a full-scale blizzard. If you're not carrying the clothes you need for all of these conditions, you're going to end up having a cold, wet, and miserable outing—at best. At worst you could be in real danger of hypothermia.

Probably the best way to dress for the trail is by wearing layered clothing—clothing that can be added to or taken off as the weather conditions change. Make sure that the clothing is breathable, that it will allow body moisture to be wicked away from your skin and escape out of the clothes. As you trek or ski, you're going to work up a sweat. The secret to staying warm is to stay dry and comfortable. Next to your skin wear long underwear that's made of polypropylene or something similar. These types of materials will wick the moisture away from your skin, allowing you to stay dry.

For the most part, the winter climate in Colorado is not a wet one. There may be snow, but it tends to stay fairly dry and cold, so the big threat is from your own sweat. During the spring, snows can be wetter. In either case a good waterproof breathable shell and pants made of Gore-Tex or some similar material are important to keep the snow from sticking to your clothes. Don't wear cotton. Snow will cling to jeans or corduroy pants and melt, making you wet. A ski hat, neck gaitor, light and heavy gloves, and gaitors (to keep snow out of your boots) are the lightest types of clothing and can be put on or taken off to maintain your comfort in cold weather.

Because weather conditions and trail conditions can change so quickly, be prepared by carrying a complete winter survival kit. At a minimum this should be a backpack loaded with the gear you might need to survive overnight. The following are some of the items that should be considered a must each and every time you hit the trail:

1. Backpack
2. One-liter water bottle or hydration pack (if you can keep the hose from freezing)
3. Shell jacket and pants
4. Knit hat
5. Neck gaitor
6. Ski goggles
7. Gloves, both light and heavy
8. Gaitors
9. Two to three thin layers such as a Polarfleece pullover and vest.
10. Sunglasses, lip balm, sunscreen
11. Map of the area and compass
12. High energy food—enough for an overnight stay
13. Waterproof matches, fire-starting material, lighter
14. Knife or multipurpose tool

15. First-aid kit

16. Flashlight with extra batteries

17. Headlamp

18. Avalanche transceiver, probe poles

19. Lightweight avalanche shovel

20. Pencil and paper

21. Plastic whistle

Other items that you might want to include are emergency signal flares, a smoke signaling device, a first-aid book, and a survival manual.

If you're planning an overnight excursion, additional items to add to your pack should include the following:

1. Foam pad—Thinsulate, Therma-Rest, or other waterproof type

2. Water filter

3. Sleeping bag in waterproof cover

4. Ground tarp

5. Tent or other shelter with extra cord

6. Extra batteries for lights and radios

7. Stove

8. Pans and kitchen utensils

9. Extra clothing

Trip Planning and Trail Safety

Although the Rocky Mountains of Colorado are beautiful, they can also be challenging. Even novice trails require more caution than going out and taking a couple of laps on the snow-covered flat track at the local nordic center. This is not to say that cross-country skiing and snowshoeing in the state is dangerous and should be avoided. Quite the contrary is true if you are properly clothed, equipped, and prepared for your backcountry adventure.

The trail descriptions and accompanying maps in this book are to be used as guides only. Exact routes and conditions will vary greatly because of use, weather conditions, trail conditions, and snow. Signs that were bright, new, and easy to see this year could have been knocked down, weathered, lost, or (this is the best) covered by snow by the time you encounter them! It's best to make sure that you have current and detailed maps, the latest avalanche information, a compass, and even a GPS receiver. It's also of paramount importance that you know how to read a map and use a compass for navigation in the backcountry.

For those who do not possess good backcountry navigation skills, practice them before going on a difficult trip. Go to a familiar place with a USGS 7.5-minute topographic map and compare what you see with what is on the map. Also practice using a compass and adjusting for the difference between north and magnetic north. It may be necessary to travel with experienced skiers for a few trips before you really understand how to use the map and compass. Check with local ski shops, ski resorts, nordic centers, the Forest Service, the Park Service, and avalanche hotlines to get the latest information before you get on the trail. If you're interested in a long and difficlut trip such as the one over Pearl Pass from Ashcroft to Crested Butte, you may want to inquire about hiring a guide.

Probably one of the greatest modern tools for the outdoor enthusiast is the Global Positioning Satellite (GPS) hand-held receiver. Developed as a military instrument for U.S. troops around the world, a GPS receiver allows a person on the ground to be able to locate the latitude and longitude coordinates anywhere on the planet by putting them in touch with a system of satellites now in orbit. Precise to less than 100 yards, the GPS coordinates can help you (if you know how to read a map with latitude/longitude coordinates) navigate in the backcountry. Keep in mind that GPS receivers often don't work or receive signals well when you are in a heavy canopied forest, so readings should be taken when you are on the top of a hill or in an open area.

Summer trails are usually well marked and well worn. In the winter, trails can be covered with deep snows and visibility can be severely limited. The old adage "if you get lost in the woods, hug a tree and wait for help" may be good for summer backcountry adventures, but it likely wouldn't be sound advice if you're lost in the winter. Being lost in winter—with or without a blizzard dumping on you—can be a very frightening experience. You had best be prepared to navigate your way to safety or at least into an area where mountain search and rescue teams can locate you.

Beginning with the basics: Make sure that somebody knows where you are going, how long you are supposed to be gone, and when you should return. That way, if you're not back when you're supposed to be, somebody can notify the proper authorities and get help organized and on its way to you.

Also be aware that these major search and rescue operations can cost tens of thousands of dollars in manpower hours and equipment. In Colorado every skier or snowshoer should consider it another "must" to purchase a Colorado Outdoor Recreation Search and Rescue Certificate (CORSAR). It costs only $3.00 and is good for the year. For this price you've just purchased the best and cheapest insurance policy of your life! If you have a valid card you are automatically covered and protected against costs incurred in all search and rescue operations. Without it the state of Colorado will still rescue or assist you with whatever emergency has happened, but then they are going to bill you for those emergency costs! If you hold a hunting or fishing license, the state will also provide rescue services free. The fee you pay for a CORSAR will not cover services outside search and rescue. Ambulance rides, treatment by paramedics, and other expenses once you are out of the woods will still be your responsibility.

In addition to the concerns about weather, it is possible to encounter avalanches even on trails with low avalanche danger ratings. Each year there are hundreds of avalanches throughout the state. Most occur naturally away from people and don't hurt anyone. Others result in injury and death to skiers, snowshoers, climbers, snowmobilers, and hikers. The best way to handle avalanches is to avoid them! That may sound silly and simplistic, but it's the best safety advice anyone can offer you. Avalanches that cause the deaths of skiers or other backcountry travelers are almost always set off by the people themselves.

Always check on avalanche conditions before you go out on any of the trails. The state of Colorado maintains a twenty-four-hour Avalanche Information Center that provides recorded and constantly updated information about all areas of the state. You should call them at (970) 668–0600 or visit the Web site, geosurvey.state.co.us/avalanche, each and every time before venturing out.

Avalanche tranceivers, probe poles, and shovels are items you must have with you at all times. When you take an organized tour or hire a snow-country guide, such gear is considered mandatory.

Here are a few safety tips to always keep in mind about avalanches in the backcountry:

1. Danger of avalanche or snowslides increases greatly on any slope with an angle at or over 30 degrees. Avoid crossing or skiing slopes that are this steep.

2. It is always safer to ski or trek along the edge of angled open areas than it is to venture out into the center.

3. Snow stability changes on an hourly basis. Signs of unstable snow include the *whoomph* sound of snow settling, heavily wind-loaded slopes on the leeward sides of hills, cornices, and signs of past avalanches, such as broken tree limbs and cleared timber.

4. New snow on top of old snow is often very unstable. In fact, most avalanches occur just after large snowstorms. Wait a day or two

Digging a snow pit to assess the avalanche danger.

after a snowstorm while the sun and warmer temperatures help stabilize the new snow as part of the existing snow pack.

5. Overhanging cornices should be avoided from both above and below in any type of weather. If you're walking out on them, they can break and take you with them. If you're underneath and they break free, they can bury you instantly.

6. When crossing a potential avalanche chute or danger area, never cross as a group. Only one person at a time should cross the area and then radio or hand signal back to the rest of the group for the next person to come across. All the members of the group should watch each person cross the dangerous section of slope. If there is an avalanche, others in the party can watch the victim and begin a rescue. It is important to start a rescue as soon as possible. The chances of survival diminish rapidly after the first few minutes of being buried.

7. Knowledge is power. Take an avalanche course. Outdoor equipment stores, community colleges, ski patrols, and many other organizations offer avalanche training to help winter backcountry travelers understand what to look for, what to avoid, and how to rescue someone caught in an avalanche. These usually incorporate both classroom time and field training for the best effect. The time and money spent will be well worth it.

Everybody falls down.

Backcountry Etiquette

Backcountry cross-country skiing and snowshoeing is one of the fastest growing segments of winter outdoor recreation. It's relatively low tech and low impact and is a great way to see the high country. With the record numbers of people on the trails in the winter comes the concern about being able to share the pristine lands with all winter users while protecting the fragile environment now and for generations to come.

Whether you are a long time resident of Colorado or a visitor, keep in mind that nobody owns the trails. They literally do belong to everyone, and for this reason everyone has a responsibility to protect them from abuse and misuse. Remember, if you're strong enough to pack all your supplies in with you, you should be strong enough to pack out your trash! Everyone is a steward for the beauty that the backcountry offers.

We hope you enjoy the beauty of the Rocky Mountains in winter, and wish you the best of outdoor winter recreation and safe journeys for years to come.

See you on the trails!

Key to Icons

cross-country skiing trail

snowshoeing trail

skate skiing (skating) trail

colorado

Lake Agnes

Colorado State Forest, Fort Collins, CO

Type of trail:	═══ 〈⚉⚉〉
Also used by:	Snowboarders.
Distance:	7 miles.
Terrain:	A short trail but steep enough to provide a challenging uphill hike to the lake, and then a great downhill run back to trailhead.
Trail difficulty:	Intermediate.
Surface quality:	Ungroomed, but often ski or snowshoe tracked.
Elevation:	The trailhead is at 9,686 feet and the hut is at 10,100 feet.
Time:	3 to 5 hours.
Avalanche danger:	Low, but some avalanche terrain is encountered.
Snowmobile use:	None.
Food and facilities:	Whether you're planning on day touring only or staying over at the Nokhu Hut, it's best to get all your groceries, gas, snacks, water, etc. before you leave the Fort Collins area. There are a lot of small roadside gas stations, a few cafes, and a few motels along Colorado Highway 14, but for the most part they are closed during the winter.

The Nokhu Hut is operated by Never Summer Nordic, Inc., and reservations for using the cabin are required in advance. For further information about availability, call (970) 482–9411. Rental costs for the cabin range from $85 to $105. The cost for the overnight stay is for your entire group, however, and represents a real bargain! There is also an additional $2.00 charge per person for state park fees. These are paid at the trailhead when you arrive.

Located within the 70,000 acres of the Colorado State Forest, the popular trail to Lake Agnes is short but is steep enough to rate as an intermediate trail. Not designed for the beginner, this trail represents a ready challenge to the experienced backcountry skier or snowshoer. Running through dense forests, the trail provides so many types of terrain that when you make it to the cabin, you will be ready for a well-deserved rest before exploring the surrounding slopes.

The Nokhu Hut, named after the Nokhu Crags to the east of the hut, is operated by Never Summer Nordic, Inc. and can accommodate up to six people for an overnight stay. The name Nokhu is thought to be an

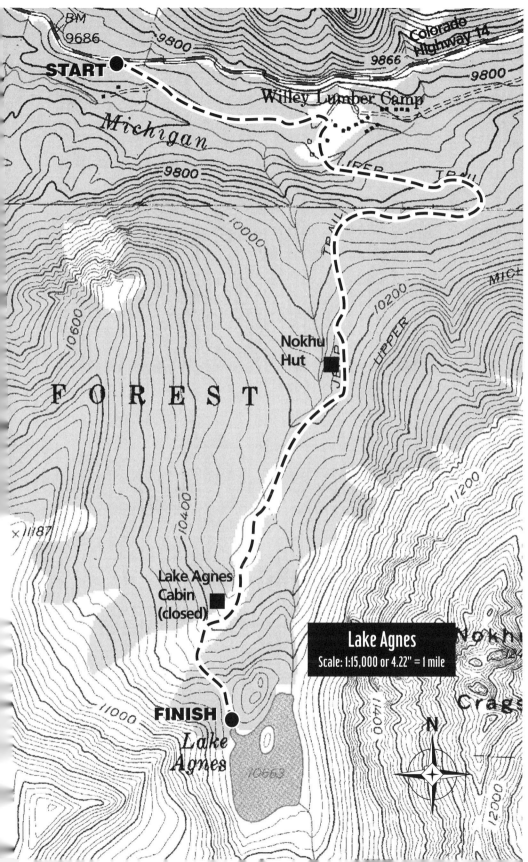

Mount Mahler and Seven Utes Mountain.

abbreviation of the Arapaho word *hohlonookee,* meaning eagle rock. This is a great place to stay for a couple of nights to explore the area around Lake Agnes, American Lakes, and Thunder Pass. A wood-burning stove supplies heat, and you obtain water by melting snow, so please don't bring any dogs.

From the Lake Agnes trailhead, head southeast on the four-wheel-drive road, crossing over a creek and climbing and dropping over a series of steep grades through a thick canopy of trees. About 0.3 mile from the trailhead, stop to pay the $2.00 day-use fee. After another 0.2 mile you'll encounter a sharp curve that veers to the south. You'll then see a fork in the road. Head right into a clearing. Turn right, cross the creek, and climb the Lake Agnes Road. Pass the entrance for Crags Campground on the right after going 0.2 mile. Stay to the right. Look for a gate on the right marked NEVER SUMMER NORDIC. Guests receive the combination to the gate when they make a reservation.

The road continues to climb steadily past the entrance to Nokhu Hut. On the right you will see Lake Agnes Cabin, which has been closed for overnight use because of its age. Climb steeply up the valley for another 0.75 mile to reach Lake Agnes.

Once you reach the lake, it's a great open area with a lot of slopes to play on. The area is becoming popular with snowboarders, who trek in on shoes and then switch to boards once they reach the lake. The area around Lake Agnes is for day use only. Winter camping is not allowed.

Directions at a glance

- The trailhead/gate to Lake Agnes is well marked with a parking area on the south side of Colorado Highway 14.

- Go through the gate and ski or snowshoe approximately 0.75 mile to a meadow.

- Take four-wheel-drive road out of the meadow to the southeast. Look for signs to Lake Agnes.

- Go 0.2 mile past Crags Campground. Continue and look for a gate to the right marked NEVER SUMMER NORDIC about 1.7 miles from the trailhead.

- Farther on, Lake Agnes Cabin will be found south of the trail. This cabin is closed.

- Go 0.5 mile from the cabin to reach Lake Agnes.

- To return follow the same route back to the trailhead.

After an afternoon of exploring, it's a fast trek or glide back down to the cabin or all the way back down to the trailhead. Steep and slow ascents up the trail to the cabin make for a wild ride back down the trail when it's time to head home!

How to get there

From Fort Collins take U.S. Highway 287 north to the junction of Colorado Highway 14. Go west on Colorado Highway 14 for approximately 60 miles to Cameron Pass. The trailhead to Lake Agnes is 2.5 miles west of Cameron Pass. The parking area is on the south side of Colorado Highway 14.

The Nokhu Hut.

Zimmerman Lake

Roosevelt National Forest, Fort Collins, CO

Type of trail: ═══ ⊙

Distance: 3.75 miles.

Terrain: A short trail with a smooth and steady ascent to lake and a fairly gentle grade back to the trailhead.

Trail difficulty: Novice to intermediate.

Surface quality: Ungroomed, but often ski or snowshoe tracked.

Elevation: The trail starts at 10,020 feet and ends at 10,495 feet.

Time: 2 to 3 hours.

Avalanche danger: Low, but the areas surrounding Montgomery Pass have avalanche hazards.

Food and facilities: It's best to get all your groceries, gas, snacks, water, etc. before you leave the Fort Collins area. There are a lot of small roadside gas stations, a few cafes, and a few motels along Colorado Highway 14, but for the most part they are closed during the winter. Once you get onto Zimmerman Lake Trail, there are no facilities.

Making tracks in the woods.

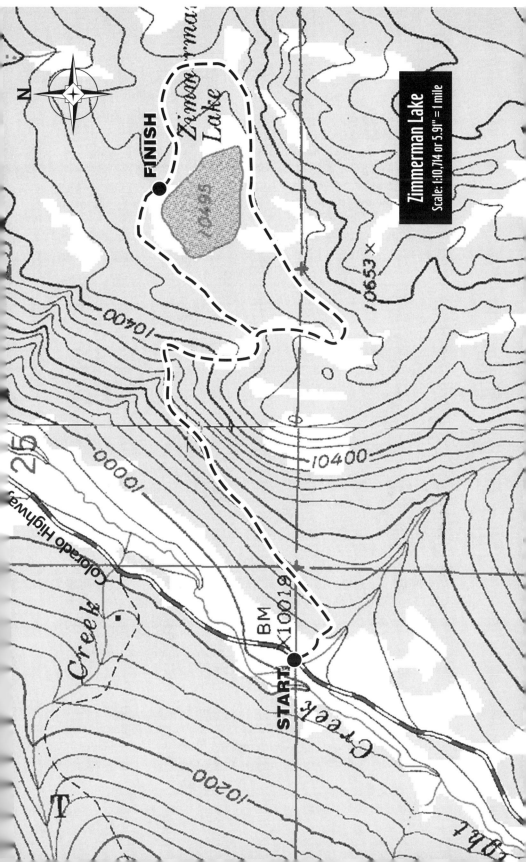

N

FINISH

Zimmerman Lake

START

BM ×10019

Creek

Colorado Highway

Creek

Creek

25

T

10400

10400

10000

10200

10495

10653 ×

Zimmerman Lake
Scale: 1:10,714 or 5.91" = 1 mile

B ecause of the steep slopes and rocky ridges of the Montgomery Pass and Cameron Pass areas, the early winter snows stick, and skiing or snowshoeing starts as early as November. The Zimmerman Lake Trail, which is popular with the locals, is a short excursion from the main road into a heavily forested area. Offering a mostly smooth, steady ascent, it has only two steep sections, one right as the trail begins and the other soon afterward at about the 0.25-mile point. Resting at the foot of cliffs that form the northern border of the Neota Wilderness Area, Zimmerman Lake offers a peaceful, solitary setting unencumbered by the mechanized traffic created by snowmobiles.

From the trailhead use the old road at the south end of the parking lot. Starting at an elevation of 10,020 feet, the trail heads southeast and climbs through a spruce/fir forest, twisting in a slight zigzag direction toward the northeast. A little after the halfway mark, the trail bends to the south for several hundred yards and then turns to the northeast again to round the northern edge of Zimmerman Lake.

Directions at a glance

- The trailhead to Zimmerman Lake begins at the parking lot.

- The trail crosses a meadow below the highway, turns left, and climbs across the hill.

- About 0.5 mile from the trailhead the trail turns right up a small gully before leveling and turning to the left toward the lake.

- Return to the trailhead on the same route you used to come in.

Alternate route

- If you want to extend your ski or snowshoe route, pick up the Loop Trail at Zimmerman Lake.

- The route can be traveled in either direction and totals another 1.75 miles.

- Use the same route to ski or snowshoe back to the trailhead.

Once you get to the lake, you may want to extend your trip by using the 1.75-mile-long Loop Trail, which goes around the lake. This loop intersects Meadows Ski Trail near the dam on Zimmerman Lake, and the Loop Trail can be easily skied or trekked in either direction. When it's time to head back to the car, just follow the same route you used coming in.

How to get there

From Fort Collins take U.S. Highway 287 north to the junction of Colorado Highway 14. Go west on Colorado Highway 14 for approximately 58 miles. Approximately 2.25 miles before you reach the top of Cameron Pass, pull off at the Zimmerman Lake parking area on the east side of the road.

Bear Lake

Rocky Mountain National Park, Estes Park, CO

Type of trail:	▬▬▬ ⬭
Also used by:	Ice anglers.
Distance:	A 0.75-mile loop around Bear Lake; 3.6-mile round trip to Nymph, Dream, and Emerald Lakes.
Terrain:	The loop around Bear Lake is flat and gentle. The trail to Nymph, Dream, and Emerald Lakes provides steady but gentle ascents.
Trail difficulty:	Novice to intermediate.
Surface quality:	Ungroomed, but often ski or snowshoe tracked.
Elevation:	Trail starts at 9,475 feet and ends at 10,230 feet.
Time:	30 minutes to 1 hour around Bear Lake loop; 3 to 4 hours round trip to Emerald Lake.
Avalanche danger:	Low.
Food and facilities:	Although Rocky Mountain National Park is a popular winter destination, there are not a lot of facilities open in the park during the cross-country skiing and snowshoeing season. There are restroom facilities at the Bear Lake area and the park's Visitor Center, but the closest food and overnight accommodations will be found in Estes Park, which has plenty of grocery stores, convenience stores, gas stations, and places to get lunches and snacks before heading into the park. For Rocky Mountain National Park information, call (970) 586–1206. It costs $15 per vehicle to enter the park, but after that there are no additional charges for using the winter recreation areas and trails.

The Estes Park Chamber and Visitor Information Center can provide skiers and snowshoers with brochures and referrals on lodging and restaurants. Call toll-free, (800) 44–ESTES (37837).

The premier hotel in Estes Park is the Stanley Hotel. Built in 1909 by Mr. F. O. Stanley—the inventor of the Stanley Steamer automobile—the historic and elegant hotel has been remodeled and renovated within the last few years. It's pricey but grand.

Established by Congress in 1915, Rocky Mountain National Park is 265,727 acres of spectacular mountain scenery, including one of the most famous Colorado fourteeners—Longs Peak at 14,255 feet. In

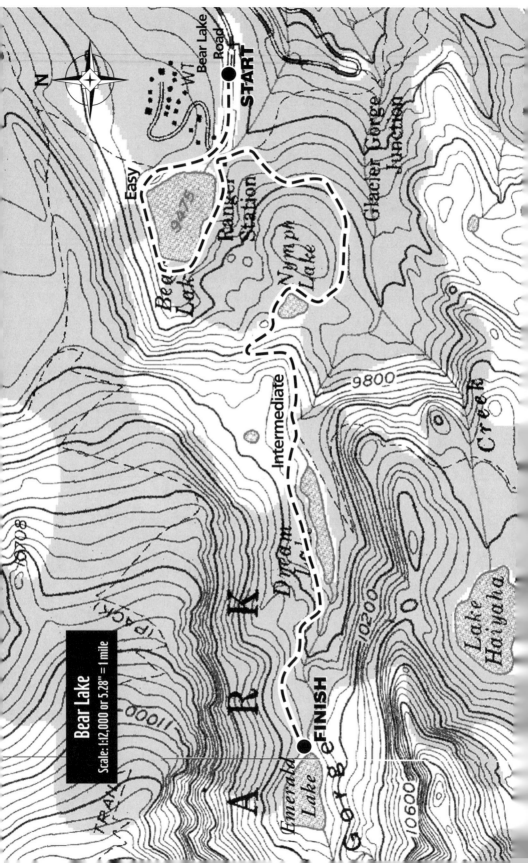

the park you might see elk, deer, and an occasional moose. During the winter months, great horned owls and Steller's jays make the park their home. Located on the east side of the Continental Divide, the park is a convenient distance for winter enthusiasts from Denver and the Front Range. Snowmobilers are only allowed on the west side access from Grand Lake and can travel on Trail Ridge Road up to Milner Pass. Snowmobile traffic is not permitted on the cross-country and snowshoe trails described here.

The route to Bear Lake is short, with only a moderate and steady climb. If the pristine views aren't enough of a reason to venture forth, then take your fishing pole and ice auger. Ice fishing at Emerald Lake can reap cutthroat, rainbow, and brown trout. Fishing is not allowed at Bear Lake. Check with the park ranger for limits and regulations.

From the parking area near Bear Lake, head north across the road and look for the well-marked trailhead. The quickest and easiest route is a short trail up to and around Bear Lake. Taking less than one hour and covering just over 0.75 mile, it's perfect for you if you are a novice skier or snowshoer. On weekends this area is pretty crowded, but if you come on weekdays, you can enjoy much more solitude.

A short distance after starting up to Bear Lake, a trail cuts off to the left that will take you 0.5-mile to Nymph Lake. Gaining 225 feet in elevation, the trail is also rated as easy. Soon after leaving Bear Lake

Directions at a glance

- The trailhead for Bear Lake begins at the parking area and is well signed.
- Follow the signs up 0.25 mile and follow the trail around the lake. It's only a 0.75-mile loop around Bear Lake, which brings you back to the trailhead.

Alternate route

- Follow the trail from the parking lot toward Bear Lake. Less than 0.13 mile from the trailhead, take the route that will direct you to Nymph, Dream, and Emerald Lakes.
- The route to Nymph Lake is approximately 0.5 mile and is rated as easy.
- From Nymph Lake the trail to Dream Lake and Emerald Lake is rated as intermediate.
- The trail from Nymph Lake to Dream Lake covers approximately 0.5 mile and climbs steadily, gaining about 300 feet in elevation.
- The trail from Dream Lake to Emerald Lake is well signed and covers another 0.5 mile with a steady climb to around 10,300 feet.
- To return to the trailhead, enjoy a gentle glide or trek back along the same route.

Trail, it forks. Take the right—or west—route, which soon winds around to the southwest and leads you to the small lake.

The trail that goes on from Nymph Lake to Dream and Emerald Lakes is rated as moderately difficult and climbs another 300 feet in elevation. From the west shore of Nymph Lake, head north on a switchback that will take you finally to the west. Keep on the right side of the gully, climbing steadily for 0.5 mile to Dream Lake.

If Dream Lake is frozen solid, you can ski or snowshoe across, but always beware that lake crossings are inherently dangerous. If the ice is too thin over the lake, head up the left side of the valley above the lake for several hundred yards. When the terrain levels, cross to the right side of the valley through the trees and continue on a little more than 0.5 mile to Emerald Lake at 10,080 feet.

How to get there

From Boulder head north and then northwest on U.S. Highway 36 approximately 31 miles to Estes Park. Drive through the town and follow U.S. Highway 36 signs to the entrance of Rocky Mountain National Park at the Beaver Meadows entrance station. Pay your $15 per vehicle day-use fee there. After entering the park, stay on the main park road for 0.25 mile, then turn left onto Bear Lake Road. Another 9 miles and it will bring you to the parking area east of Bear Lake.

Bear Lake to Fern Lake

Rocky Mountain National Park, Estes Park, CO

Type of trail:

Distance: 5 miles one way to Fern Lake; 10 miles one way to Moraine Park (shuttle vehicle required for return trip).

Terrain: Challenging climbs and descents all along the route.

Trail difficulty: Advanced.

Surface quality: The first 2 miles are ungroomed but often ski or snowshoe tracked. The rest of the trail is ungroomed backcountry conditions.

Elevation: Bear Lake trailhead is at 9,475 feet. Fern Lake is at 9,530 feet. Moraine Park Trail ends at 8,200 feet.

Time: 2 days.

Avalanche danger: Low to moderate. Avalanche chutes exist along the way, and extreme caution should always be taken.

Food and facilities: Although Rocky Mountain National Park is a popular winter destination, there are not a lot of facilities open in the park during the cross-country skiing and snowshoeing season. There are restroom facilities at the Bear Lake area and the park's Visitor Center. You'll find the closest food and overnight accommodations in Estes Park, which has plenty of grocery stores, convenience stores, gas stations, and places to get lunches and snacks before heading into the park. For Rocky Mountain National Park information, call (970) 586–1206. It costs $15 per vehicle to enter the park, but after that there are no additional charges for using the winter recreation areas and trails.

If you're going all the way to Moraine Park, you're going to have to plan on leaving a shuttle vehicle at the end of the trail.

The Estes Park Chamber and Visitor Information Center can provide you with brochures and referrals on lodging and restaurants. Call toll-free, (800) 44–ESTES (37837).

The premier hotel in Estes Park is the Stanley Hotel. Built in 1909 by F. O. Stanley—the inventor of the Stanley Steamer automobile—the historic and elegant hotel has been remodeled and renovated within the last few years. It's pricey but grand.

ocky Mountain National Park offers 415 square miles of untamed forests, valleys, and mountain areas for the cross-country skier and snowshoer. All are a relatively short distance from metro Denver and the Front Range. Even in the wintertime Moraine Park Campground is open for tent and RV camping, while Longs Peak Campground is open to tent camping only. There is a $10 fee for camping in these sites. There's no firewood in the park, and campers must bring their own water. But an overnight adventure on one of the unmarked trails is truly worth the experience for skiers or snowshoers who are familiar with Colorado's temperamental weather conditions and are experienced in reading topographical maps.

Winter camping gear, food, maps, and a compass are a must for this route. A GPS receiver can also be useful if you know how to use it. This trail from Bear Lake begins as an easy hike or glide. But soon after skiing or snowshoeing off the beginner route, the trail is long and difficult. Follow this path and the snow is usually consistent for skiing or snowshoeing. You may find snow waist deep in the higher elevations.

The beauty and challenge of Bear Lake/Moraine Park Trail lies in staying overnight along the trail in primitive winter conditions. Although carving out an overnight snow cave is an option, preparing for a comfortable overnight winter stay with tents, sleeping bags, lanterns or flashlights,

Taking skins off after a climb.

Directions at a glance

- The trailhead for Bear Lake begins at the parking area and is well signed.
- Go north 0.13 mile on Bear Lake Trail, then right to intersect Flattop Mountain Trail.
- At 0.5 mile the trail will turn left and start heading west.
- At 0.75 mile take the trail to the northwest that's marked as the route to Fern Lake.
- At about 2.5 miles, you'll reach Marigold Pond, then Two Rivers Lake, and then Lake Helene. From this point topo maps and a compass are necessary.
- The trail makes a hard right turn and treks north along the base of Joe Mills Mountain and along the edge of Odessa Lake. This is a potential avalanche area, so use caution.
- Ski or trek downhill for the next 1 mile, and you'll reach Fern Lake.
- Fern Lake is about the halfway point and a good area to set up your overnight winter camp.
- Follow the summer trail marked to The Pool from the east side of Fern Lake.
- The trail goes downhill in a north and northeast direction along Fern Lake.
- Cross Pool Bridge where Fern Creek and Big Thompson River merge.
- Continue along the trail to the east for the next couple of miles following the signs to Moraine Park.
- Pick up a shuttle vehicle at Moraine Park and drive back to the Bear Lake trailhead to retrieve your other car.

freeze-dried foods, and self-contained stoves and fire-starters can make it a memorable overnight adventure.

Ski or snowshoe around the east edge of Bear Lake for about 0.1 mile and turn north to intersect Flattop Mountain Trail. You'll ski or snowshoe east over a flat switchback that'll steer you over a small hill dotted with aspens, until you are finally heading west (or to your left). About 0.5 mile from the trailhead, you'll climb to the top of the ridge, contouring along a broad valley to the north and west, while staying on the right side of the stream.

Heading west, continue through the woods, passing a trail junction on your left at about the 0.75-mile mark. Veer to the right or northwest, climbing steadily. You can follow the summer trail, but some of it is on a steep slope and the snow cover is occasionally poor. Continue to follow the basic route, but seek out the best trail. *Exercise caution:* There is some potential avalanche danger in the area. You should have avalanche beacons, shovels, and the latest updates on avalanche conditions.

At about the 2.25-mile point, you will reach Marigold Pond and then Two Rivers Lake to the south. From this point the trail is not well marked and topo maps and a compass are a must. A handheld GPS receiver is a bonus to take you farther along the trail.

If you want to do a little flat-ski skating or snow trekking, test the ice thickness on Two Rivers Lake, and if it's thick enough, ski or snowshoe around and across it. If you're dropping down low to the lake level, ski or snowshoe across it, heading west a short distance to Lake Helene.

After the fun on the "flat stuff," head to your right going north to Odessa Gorge. Climb the ridge between Odessa Gorge and Lake Helene for a short distance to the first small break in the ridgeline. Traverse to the right as you descend and look uphill to the top of Joe Mills Mountain to again assess the possible avalanche danger. Chutes abound in this area, as well as unstable snow. If it's safe, enjoy a thrilling downhill run. Once you're down, you'll see that the right side of the valley leads naturally to Odessa Lake at about 3.5 miles from the start of the trail.

Follow the narrow gorge, staying to the right of the streambed for the next 0.25 mile. Cross the stream, then follow it down to the left side, bending slightly away to the left as you do so. The terrain grows steep, and you can downhill one more time before the route curves to the east, or right, toward Fern Lake. If you want to stay overnight for your winter camping excursion in this area, the Fern Lake area is a lot less windy and more comfortable than Odessa Gorge.

After overnighting in the region of Fern Lake, you have about a 5-mile mostly, downhill trek. Following the summer trail with its excellent signage from the east side of Fern Lake, you'll drop quickly through a series of switchbacks that ultimately continue east to The Pool on the Big Thompson River. Cross Pool Bridge and continue on the trail for the last 3 miles, dropping gradually along the valley, following the signs to Moraine Park. It is considered rare to ski or snowshoe out from the Pool Bridge.

Reach the Moraine Park area and pick up the shuttle vehicle that you parked on the trail.

How to get there

From Boulder head north and then northwest on U.S. Highway 36 approximately 31 miles to Estes Park. Drive through the town and follow U.S. Highway 36 signs to the entrance of Rocky Mountain National Park at the Beaver Meadows entrance station. Pay your $15 per vehicle day-use fee there. After entering the park, stay on the main park road for 0.25 mile and then turn left onto Bear Lake Road. After another 9 miles, you will reach the parking area east of Bear Lake.

Service Creek

Service Creek State Wildlife Area, Steamboat Springs, CO

Type of trail:	━━ ●
Distance:	11.5 miles.
Terrain:	Gradual, but continual climbs to the end of the trail and then gentle glide or trek back to the trailhead.
Trail difficulty:	Intermediate to advanced.
Surface quality:	Ungroomed backcountry conditions.
Elevation:	The trailhead is at 7,000 feet, and you will climb to 7,840 feet.
Time:	2 to 5 hours.
Avalanche danger:	Low to moderate.
Food and facilities:	Gas, food, drinks, and all equipment needs should definitely be taken care of before leaving Steamboat Springs. Very few winter facilities are available outside town. Because you're going into a true wilderness area, everything has to be packed in. Plan on being self-sufficient.

Because the Service Creek State Wildlife Area (SWA) is so remote, for the latest conditions on snow, avalanche dangers, and road closures in the area, call the Stagecoach State Recreation Area (970–736–2436).

For information about lodging in Steamboat Springs, call the Steamboat Springs Chamber of Commerce at (970) 879–0880 or visit the Web site: www.steamboat-chamber.com.

In the winter months the SWA is closed because it is a major wintering area for herds of Rocky Mountain elk and deer. No vehicles are allowed. However, it is open to cross-country skiers or snowshoers looking for a pristine and uncrowded wilderness area that provides some great winter wildlife viewing.

The trail is very popular during the spring, summer, and fall, but nearly abandoned during the snow season. The isolation makes this a trail offering a great deal of backcountry beauty and the experience of skiing into a true wilderness area. Because the area beyond the Service Creek trailhead is a designated wilderness area, no mechanized travel is allowed: no snowmobiles, no ATVs, and not even mountain bikers.

From where you park your car at the winter closure on County Road 18, follow the road along the Yampa River to the Service Creek trailhead, located where Service Creek joins the Yampa River from the southeast. Pick up Trail 1105 and begin to climb steadily along the south side of Ser-

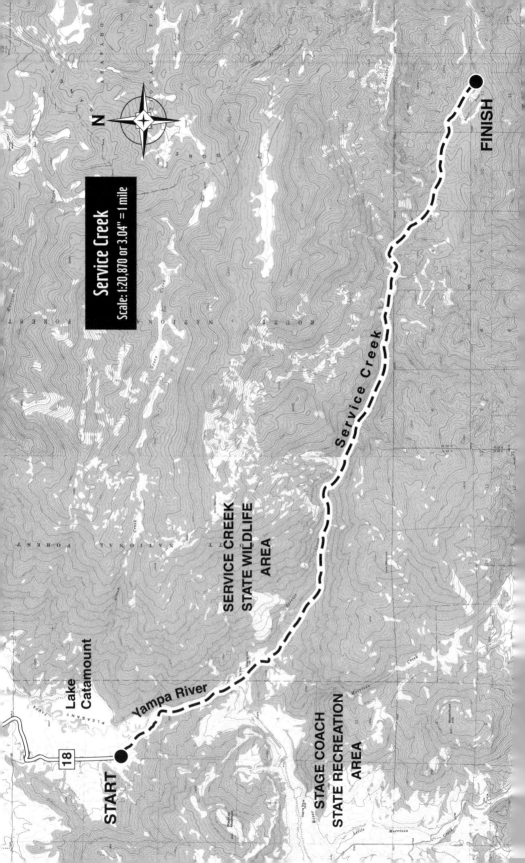

N

Service Creek
Scale: 1:20,870 or 3.04" = 1 mile

FINISH

Service Creek

SERVICE CREEK
STATE WILDLIFE
AREA

Lake Catamount

Yampa River

18

START

STAGE COACH
STATE RECREATION
AREA

vice Creek. Although rated at an intermediate ability level, this trail requires a lot of climbing and is recommended for skiers and snowshoers who are in good physical condition. The ancient forests of conifers are mature and grand and virtually untouched by humans.

Just over 2.2 miles from the Service Creek trailhead, you'll come to an old bridge that crosses the creek. This is a natural spot to stop, rest, and take in the natural beauty and silence that surrounds you. Service Creek has more than a few small waterfalls that freeze solid in the colder winter months. Cascading ice sheets and strange water sculptures can make for some great and very unusual photo opportunities. Hiking or skiing back out from this point is a lot less physically taxing, and the downhill runs provide a much quicker trip back to the Service Creek trailhead. From here follow County Road 18 back to your car.

How to get there

Take U.S. Highway 40 south from Steamboat Springs approximately 2 miles to Colorado Highway 131. Then take Colorado Highway 131 to the Lake Catamount sign and turn left onto County Road 18. Turn left at the junction of County Road 18 and County Road 148, following County Road 18 until you reach the snow closure. Park out of the way of other trail users.

Rabbit Ears Pass

Routt National Forest, Steamboat Springs, CO

Type of trail:	▬▬ 🔘
Also used by:	Snowmobilers.
Distance:	5 miles.
Terrain:	Gentle but constant climb to the top of the peak and gentle glide or trek back to trailhead.
Trail difficulty:	Intermediate.
Surface quality:	Ungroomed, but usually tracked by skiers or snowshoers.
Elevation:	The trailhead is at 9,600 feet, and you will climb to 10,651 feet.
Time:	3 hours.
Avalanche danger:	Low to moderate.
Snowmobile use:	Moderate to high.
Food and facilities:	Winter services in the area are sparse at best. Fuel up your vehicle, check your equipment, and purchase your drinks, sack lunches, and supplies before leaving Steamboat Springs. The city of Steamboat Springs has great restaurants, grocery and liquor stores, and ski and snowshoe shops and rentals, as well as plenty of motels and bed-and-breakfast accommodations. Call for information about Steamboat Springs and adventures in the area (970–879–0880), or use the Web site, www.steamboat-chamber.com.

Throughout the winter months, the snow is plentiful in this region and allows the outdoor enthusiast excellent opportunities to ski or snowshoe from early to late in the season. If cross-country ski touring is your passion, the gently rolling terrain, open meadows, and variety of trails are ideal. Most of the terrain is rated at an intermediate skill level.

Named for the large two-rock formation that stands on the northeast side of the wide flat area at its summit, Rabbit Ears Pass is a wonderland of great winter terrain. Most of the ski and snowshoe designated terrain is on the western side of the pass beginning from three parking areas: Walton Creek, Fox Curve, and West Summit. This is an area that should be relatively free of snowmobilers, who are allowed to ride farther east on the pass.

To begin the West Summit Loops 1A and 1B, follow the blue diamonds from the parking lot until the trail comes to a T-junction, then turn left to the west. Follow the trail over gently rolling terrain before climbing to a telephone line. Soon after passing under the wires, the trail

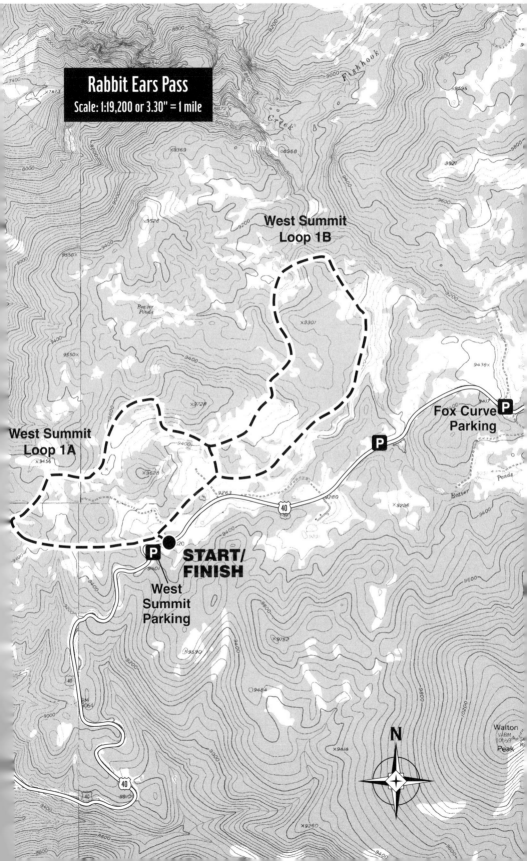

turns back to the right and meanders up a ridge to a spot where you can descend into an easy bowl. If you feel up to it, make a few laps by climbing back to the top and descending again. At the bottom follow the trail to the junction with West Summit Loop 1B, which heads off to the left. Go another short distance and Loop 1B intersects the trail again. From here turn right to reach the junction with the spur to the parking lot. If you want to extend your tour, follow West Summit Loop 1B from the first junction and back. The distance is about 4 miles.

As well as the West Summit Loops, there are four other tours available for cross-country skiing and snowshoeing at the top of Rabbit Ears Pass. The South Summit Loop is a 3-mile loop that leaves from the south side of U.S. Highway 40 at the West Summit parking area. It also connects to the challenging Par-a-lel Route, which leads to the North Walton Peak Route, both of which begin at the Walton Creek trailhead. Walton Peak is the farthest east the Forest Service recommends skiers and snowshoers go on the pass.

Across the highway on the north side are the 3-mile Fox Curve Loop, leaving from its own parking lot, and Bruce's Trail, a 3.1-mile trail that winds back and forth through the woods just east of the West Summit lot. The most challenging of the ski tours on Rabbit Ears Pass is the Hogan Park Route, which crosses the open meadows, called parks, north of the highway to the top of Mount Werner, where Steamboat Resort is located. This is a very challenging tour because of the demanding route finding. A guide or someone in the group who has made the trip is strongly recommended. Also be sure to bring safety straps. You will be required to use them while skiing down from the top of Steamboat.

How to get there

The designated cross-country skiing and snowshoeing areas on Rabbit Ears Pass are about 13 miles east of Steamboat Springs. From town take U.S. Highway 40 south and then east to the West Summit parking area.

Directions at a glance

- Ski a short distance from the parking lot to the junction of West Summit Loop 1A.

- Turn left going west onto the trail and ski 1 mile until you pass under a telephone line. Soon after, the trail turns sharply to the east.

- Go another 1.0 mile to the top of a small bowl where you can ski down.

- At about 0.5 mile from the bottom of the bowl, West Summit Loop 1B goes to the left. After about 0.25 mile there is a second junction with West Summit Loop 1B to the left.

- Return to the parking lot via the short trail you came in on.

Brainard Lake

Brainard Lake Recreation Area, Ward, CO

Type of trail:	▬▬ 🎿
Distance:	2.2 miles to 5.4 miles.
Terrain:	Rolling hills with gentle climbs and descents.
Trail difficulty:	Novice.
Surface quality:	Ungroomed, but usually tracked by skiers or snowshoers.
Elevation:	The trail starts at 10,080 feet and the lake is at 10,345 feet.
Time:	3 hours.
Avalanche danger:	Low.
Food and facilities:	Located less than 35 miles from downtown Boulder, Brainard Lake is an ideal day-trip location. If you're planning on making Brainard Cabin your overnight destination, advance reservations are a must! You must also be a member of the Colorado Mountain Club (CMC). It's easy to join and costs you a $25 initiation fee and then $41 per year to maintain your membership. At least one member of your party must be a member to reserve the cabin, which then rents for as little as $10 per night, per person. For information about joining the CMC, call (303) 554–7688.

Whether you're planning on staying overnight in the Brainard Cabin or just planning a day trip, you'll find that most of the grocery stores, convenience stores, gas stations, restaurants, and overnight accommodations are in Boulder. Contact the Boulder Chamber of Commerce at (303) 442–1044 for brochures and additional information.

In Nederland, only 4.5 miles to the south, you will find a couple of small restaurants and cafes and a twenty-four-room log hotel called the Lodge at Nederland (800–279–9463). Nederland is also a good roadside stop for last minute snacks, a cup of coffee, or lunch. |

Often described as the most popular area for cross-country skiing and snowshoeing in all of the Front Range, the Brainard Lake area has a great variety of trails for both cross-country skiers and snowshoers. Brainard Lake Trail, Waldrop North Ski Trail, CMC South Ski Trail, and Little Raven Ski Trail all leave from the Red Rock Lake trailhead and lead to Brainard Lake. There are also connections to South Saint Vrain Trail and the continuation of Little Raven Ski Trail. This system makes a great

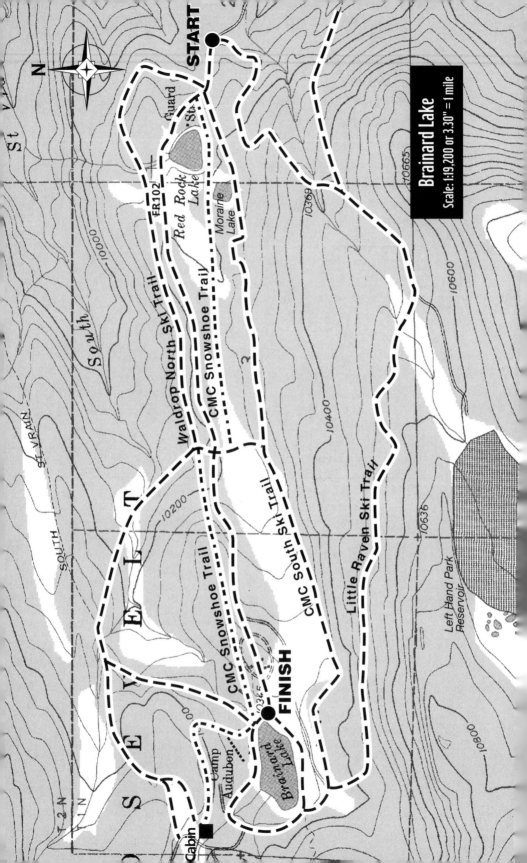

Brainard Lake
Scale: 1:19,200 or 3.30" = 1 mile

START

FINISH

N

Guard St.

Red Rock Lake

FR102

Moraine Lake

10369

Waldrop North Ski Trail

CMC Snowshoe Trail

St Vrain

South

St Vrain

South

SOUTH

10000

10200

ROOSEVELT

10400

10600

10665

CMC South Ski Trail

Little Raven Ski Trail

10636

Left Hand Park Reservoir

10800

CMC Snowshoe Trail

Camp Audubon

Brainard Lake

10345

Cabin

T 2 N
T 1 N

place for both day trips and overnight adventures. To the west the 73,391-acre Indian Peaks Wilderness Area offers unlimited access to valleys carved by ancient glaciers and bowls that tempt the telemark skier and snowshoer looking for an extended tour and slopes to hike and ski.

The easiest route to Brainard Lake is to follow Brainard Lake Road (Forest Road 102). The only route where dogs are allowed, it climbs gently for 2.2 miles to the lake. Because of the road's exposure to the weather, the snow conditions can be icy, and sometimes the wind blows the snow off it entirely.

Beginners who are looking for a trail experience should use the CMC South Ski Trail. About 30 yards past the Left Hand Park Reservoir Road, follow the blue diamond blazes right onto the trail. Soon after a snowshoe trail branches to the left. Climb for about 0.2 mile to a right-hand fork leading steeply to Brainard Lake Road. One hundred yards past the spur, the snowshoe trail crosses and continues to the right. Just past the snowshoe trail, a trail forks to the left leading to Left Hand Park Reservoir Road. For the next 2 miles, the trail is mostly level to Brainard Lake. At times the trail follows an old ditch, which can hold water early in the season. About 1.25 miles from the trailhead, a spur to the right leads to Brainard Lake Road and Waldrop North Ski Trail farther on. Just before the lake the trail climbs steeply. Little Raven Trail joins the CMC South Ski Trail from the left just before the lake. The trail then crosses an open swamp before reaching Brainard Lake Road south of the lake.

Waldrop North Ski Trail is a more difficult route to Brainard Lake, with rolling sections and places where the trail traverses hills. The trail begins just past the turnoff for CMC South Ski Trail. It skirts around a small hill then follows the clearing for an old power line. The trail climbs and descends several hills before reaching the junction of the left-hand spur that leads to Brainard Lake Road. Watch for rocky sections on these hills early in the season. Past this junction, the trail enters the trees and crosses South Saint Vrain Creek. The bridge here may be easier to use early in the season before the creek has iced over. After climbing a long hill, the trail meets South Saint Vrain Trail. Turn left and cross the creek again, then climb a short steep hill. Brainard Lake Cutoff to the left leads to the lake. Staying right the trail goes about 0.5 mile to where South Saint Vrain Trail forks to the right. Waldrop Trail to the left leads to the CMC Brainard Cabin about 0.25 mile away.

Brainard Cabin was built in 1928 and is owned and operated today by the Boulder chapter of the CMC. The two-story cabin, heated by a fireplace and a wood-burning cookstove, can accommodate up to ten people. As is usual with all backcountry cabins and huts, water is obtained by melting snow. To use this hut at least one member of your group must be an active member of the CMC. Some weekends a host is available to offer hot drinks for a small fee.

Little Raven Trail also leaves the Red Rocks Lake trailhead and is the most difficult of the three trails. Follow Sourdough Trail from just east of the Left Hand Park Reservoir Road closure. The trail follows the contour for 0.5 mile until it turns right and begins to climb steeply through the trees. Turn left on Left Hand Park Reservoir Road 0.5 mile, then turn right when the trail leaves the road. The trail then crosses the creek and descends to where it meets CMC South Ski Trail.

To protect the cross-country trails, a new snowshoe trail has been developed to allow snowshoers a place to hike. From the Left Hand Park Reservoir Road closure, the snowshoe trail follows the CMC South Ski Trail for a short distance before turning left. About 0.25 mile farther it crosses CMC South Ski Trail again. A second snowshoe trail begins on the left side of Brainard Lake Road across from Waldrop Trail, just past the closure. This trail joins the first trail about 0.2 mile from the road. The snowshoe trail then passes between Red Rock Lake and the pond to the southwest, Moraine Lake. It crosses the trail that connects CMC South Ski Trail and Brainard Lake Road after going about 1 mile. It joins the road and follows the trail that leads to Waldrop North Ski Trail briefly before turning left along the ridge parallel to the road. The trail descends off the ridge and crosses the Brainard Lake outlet on the road, then follows Brainard Lake Cutoff for 0.1 mile. Turn left and follow the trail 0.1 mile to the CMC Cabin Cutoff and the cabin.

If you're not quite ready to return and want to explore more of the area, ski the loop that circles Brainard Lake, or try one of the myriad of other routes intertwined with the network of trails to Brainard Lake.

Directions at a glance

- The trail begins at the parking area at the end of Forest Road 102.

- Take the trail west from the parking lot along the road to Red Rock Lake or take any one of the many trails that head west.

- At approximately 2 miles from the trailhead, you'll see several cabins and huts. Continue to trek or ski west to the edge of Brainard Lake.

- At Brainard Lake, the trail forks. Take the trail to the right, north and west around the north shore of the lake if the cabin is your destination. You'll see plenty of signs.

- Or if you want to loop around Brainard Lake, take either of the trails.

- To return to the trailhead, follow the same route you came in on or enjoy many of the parallel trails.

Mitchell Lake is well suited to intermediate skiers, Blue Lake is more for advanced skiers, and Long Lake is for novices.

How to get there

From Boulder go west approximately 17 miles on Colorado Highway 119 to Nederland. Once you've driven into the middle of the town, make a right on Colorado Highway 72 and go north approximately 15 miles to the town of Ward. Just north of Ward take the turnoff and go left on the road to Brainard Lake Recreation Area. It's well marked as Forest Road 102. Drive on this paved road west for 2.5 miles to where the road is closed for the winter and blocked by a gate. You'll see an area to park near the snow closure gate.

Middle Saint Vrain

Allens Park, Peaceful Valley, CO

Type of trail:	▬▬ ⬭
Also used by:	Snowmobilers.
Distance:	16 miles.
Terrain:	Gentle but constant climb up the trail. Steep climbs after the wilderness boundary.
Trail difficulty:	Novice to intermediate.
Surface quality:	Ungroomed, but usually tracked by skiers and snowshoers.
Elevation:	The trail starts at 8,600 feet and ends at 11,332 feet at Lake Gibraltar.
Time:	Full day.
Avalanche danger:	Low to moderate.
Snowmobile use:	There is snowmobile traffic in the Middle Saint Vrain Valley until you cross into the Indian Peaks Wilderness Area at 4.8 miles from the trailhead.
Food and facilities:	The Middle Saint Vrain Trail has few if any nearby facilities. It is located about 35 miles from Longmont and Boulder, where most of the grocery stores, convenience stores, gas stations, restaurants, and overnight accommodations are going to be found. It's best to plan on making advance overnight accommodations in either of these two cities. Contact the Boulder Chamber of Commerce at (303) 442–1044 for brochures and additional information.

The Indian Peaks of the Colorado Front Range are some of the most dramatic mountains in the state. With their soaring rocky peaks and broad-shouldered flanks, these mountains offer incredible recreational opportunities close to Boulder and Denver. The trail parallels Middle Saint Vrain Road as it heads west over the valley floor of Middle Saint Vrain Creek, entering a deep ravine in alpine forests before entering the Indian Peaks Wilderness Area. At the end of the trail, Saint Vrain Glacier Trail begins and stretches several miles into the wilderness. This trail ends at the high-meadow Gibraltar Lake, where you'll stare, wide-eyed, at the magnificent swirling ice sculptures of the Saint Vrain Glaciers. It is also possible to climb away from the bottom of the valley to Buchanan Pass on the Continental Divide below Sawtooth Mountain and look west over the broad open valley of Middle Park.

Snowshoeing up the Middle Saint Vrain Valley.

Technically only novice skills are necessary to ski up the Saint Vrain Valley. The trail becomes more difficult when you get above treeline, where you will encounter harsher weather conditions and steeper slopes. It's a long way to the end of Middle Saint Vrain Road, and past it the trail is remote and seldom used. Even days after a fresh snow, you may need to break trail.

Part of the beauty of Middle Saint Vrain Creek Trail is that you can turn back along the route whenever you want and glide or trek gently down to the trailhead. But for those who venture all the way to the end of the trail, the remote valley, the ice cirques of the glaciers, and Elk Tooth Mountain at 12,848 feet make the inspiring trip more than worth the effort.

From the parking area, head west through Middle Saint Vrain Campground and across the creek. Turn left onto Buchanan Pass Trail 0.1 mile from the trailhead. Because Middle Saint Vrain Road is windy and snowmobiles are allowed up to the wilderness boundary, it's best to stay off the road. The trail shadows the road for most of the way up the valley. Sourdough Trail turns to the left about 0.5 mile after the trail turns off the road. Soon afterward another trail leads to Camp Dick Campground. Another 0.5 mile along, the trail returns to the road and crosses Middle Saint Vrain Creek on a bridge. The trail then travels along the north side of the creek opposite the road. You will pass Timberline Falls and, 1 mile later, cross into an open swamp. Travel about 0.5 mile over the swamp to the old bridge that leads back to the main road. It is about 1 mile to the wilderness boundary where the road becomes the Middle Saint Vrain Trail.

Here no form of mechanized travel is permitted. Alone with the trees and snow, you'll encounter one relatively steep hill, cross a stream, and intersect another trail at the northern end of a meadow. Entering back into the woods, you'll head northwest over more level terrain for the next 2.0 miles, skiing or snowshoeing along the southwest corner of Saint Vrain Mountain. On the north side of the valley, the slopes become noticeably more rugged and craggy. At about 7.5 miles in, there'll be a fork in the road. Take the right fork, heading more north and west.

Buchanan Pass Trail turns to the left. If you decide to go this way be

Directions at a glance

- Park at the end of the plowed area west of Colorado Highway 72.
- Turn left onto Buchanan Pass Trail 0.1 mile from the trailhead.
- After 0.5 mile cross the creek using the bridge belonging to the road. The trail then follows the north side of the creek opposite the road.
- Pass Timberline Falls and 1 mile later cross into an open swamp.
- Go 0.5 mile to a bridge and return to Middle Saint Vrain Road
- At just under 5 miles from the trailhead, look for signs indicating that you are entering Indian Peaks Wilderness Area.
- About 0.25 mile into the wilderness area, you'll climb a relatively steep hill and cross a stream.
- Head northwest over the next 2 miles of level terrain to the southwest corner of Saint Vrain Mountain. The road ends at just under 8.0 miles from the trailhead. Buchanan Pass Trail turns left heading south and traverses the left-hand slope of the valley until it reaches the flatter bowl below Sawtooth Mountain. Buchanan Pass is to the right of the mountain. If you're a novice skier or snowshoer, you may want to turn around at this point. If not, plan on breaking your own trail as you continue.
- If you continue along the valley, about 9.5 miles from the trailhead, you'll ascend the open slopes to see Lake Gibraltar and the Elk Tooth Mountain.
- Contour around Lake Gibraltar and enjoy the magnificent views of Elk Tooth Mountain as well as the Saint Vrain Glaciers.
- Return to the trailhead using the same route you used to come into the area.

careful of avalanches. You will need to bring avalanche beacons and shovels if you plan to go to Buchanan Pass. This trail will traverse across the slope left of the trail until it reaches the flatter floor of the bowl below Sawtooth Mountain. Buchanan Pass is to the right of it. This is a good turnaround point if you are a beginner skier or snowshoer who doesn't want to continue on and have to break trail. If you feel adventurous, however, continue to follow the creek west. You will climb over two steep hills that are back to back. At about the 9.5-mile point, you'll break out of the trees and ascend up the open slopes, looking out over the incredible vistas of Elk Tooth Mountain.

The trail now bends around to the southwest and climbs up the last set of steep slopes to Lake Gibraltar at 11,332 feet. Before you, at the head of the valley, are the indescribable Saint Vrain Glaciers, stretching to the Continental Divide.

After some breathtaking views and some great photo opportunities, you follow the same route for the return trip to the road and trailhead. As you might imagine, it's somewhat quicker because you can follow your tracks and ski slightly downhill all the way back to your car.

How to get there

From Boulder go west approximately 17 miles on Colorado Highway 119 to Nederland. Turn right onto Colorado Highway 72 and go approximately 15 miles to Ward. Continue on Colorado Highway 72 for 6 miles to Peaceful Valley. At the west side of Peaceful Valley, Colorado Highway 72 curves south and then heads east. At the far western end, look for the signs to the Saint Vrain campground. Park in a plowed area west of Colorado Highway 72. If the parking lot is not plowed, be sure to park legally on Colorado Highway 72.

Lost Lake

Roosevelt National Forest, Nederland, CO

Type of trail:	
Also used by:	Snowmobilers.
Distance:	6 miles.
Terrain:	Gentle climbs and descents with lots of open areas.
Trail difficulty:	Novice to intermediate.
Surface quality:	Ungroomed, but usually well tracked by skiers or snowshoers.
Elevation:	The trail starts at 8,810 feet and ends at Lost Lake, elevation 9,780 feet.
Time:	3 to 4 hours.
Avalanche danger:	Low.
Snowmobile use:	Moderate.
Food and facilities:	Located less than 30 miles from downtown Boulder, Eldora Mountain Resort and Lost Lake Trail are ideal day-trip locations. You'll find grocery stores, convenience stores, gas stations, restaurants, and overnight accommodations in Boulder. Contact the Boulder Chamber of Commerce at (303) 442–1044 for brochures and additional information.

In Nederland, you will find a couple of small restaurants and a twenty-four-room log hotel called the Lodge at Nederland (800–279–9463). Nederland also has a couple of small independent motels and bed-and-breakfast facilities. It's also a good roadside stop for last minute snacks, a cup of coffee, or lunch.

Eldora Mountain Resort is located just minutes from the Lost Lake trailhead. At the resort there's a full cafeteria and cocktail lounge. There are no overnight facilities at the resort, so plan accordingly. They do have a full line of cross-country ski and snowshoe rentals, however. Call (303) 440–8700 for additional information.

Popular because of its proximity to Denver and Boulder, this area is laced with trails. The tour to Lost Lake is a fun outing for any level skier or snowshoer who wants to enjoy the beauty of a high-elevation mountain lake. Well tracked, not too long, and with manageable elevation gains, this tour is ideal for beginners who want to discover the sport of

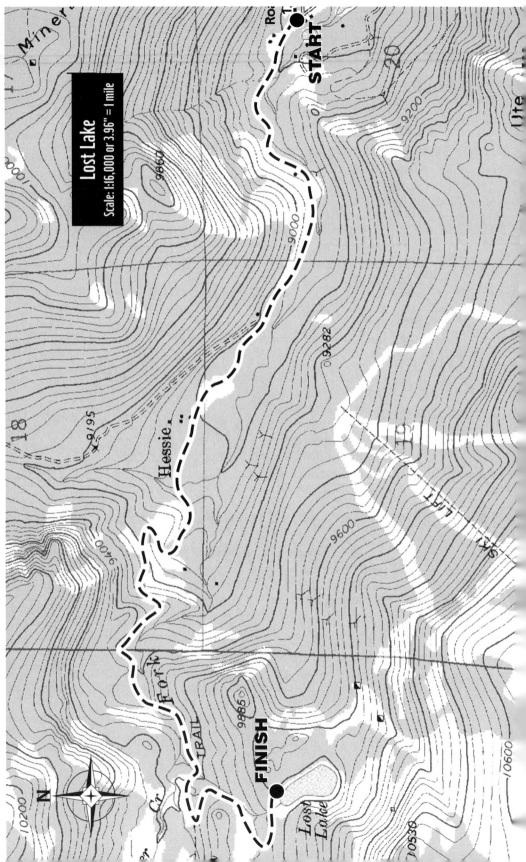

Lost Lake
Scale: 1:16,000 or 3.96" = 1 mile

START

FINISH

Lost Lake

Hessie

N

9282

9885

9860

9600

9400

9200

9000

10200

10400

10600

Mineral

Ute

Roa

cross-country skiing, or for snowshoers who want to take a pleasant walk without losing their breath. Only a couple sections of the trail, especially the last one that actually leads to the lake, offer fairly steep hills. Snowshoers will think it's a breeze.

From the unplowed road at the parking area, ski or snowshoe west. The road winds, alternating between sections heading northwest and then dipping to the south and then veering northwest again. At the 1-mile point, you'll see a fork in the road going north. Choose the fork to the left, or west. It is well marked with a sign for Hessie Road. Continue on to descend into the valley of the South Fork of Boulder Creek. Soon you'll come to the old townsite of Hessie. The entire Eldora area at the base of Ute Mountain was once a hard rock mining community. Remnants of old gold and silver mines dot the backcountry throughout the area.

Continue west past Hessie, cross over the North Fork of Middle Boulder Creek, and then maneuver over a series of sharp turns that switchback up a moderately steep hill. Beginners will be happy that the trail flattens out at about the 2-mile point. Traversing a vehicle bridge, you'll cross over the South Fork of Middle Boulder Creek, climb moderately through a clearing, and see the trail marker to Lost Lake at a little over 2.5 miles from the trailhead.

From this trail junction go south (left). The final portion of Lost Lake Trail is only 0.5 mile in length and will climb up a hillside through the trees. You'll pass another fork; again, go south. The trail will

Directions at a glance

- The parking and trailhead will be at the end of County Road 130 where the snow closure is located.

- Take the trail west along the road for approximately 1 mile.

- The trail will fork at the 1-mile point. Take the fork to the left, heading west. Watch for signs indicating Hessie Road.

- Descend into the valley along the South Fork of Middle Boulder Creek and ski or snowshoe to the townsite of Hessie.

- Continue west past Hessie, crossing over the North Fork of Middle Boulder Creek.

- The trail climbs and then flattens out about 2 miles from the trailhead.

- Traverse a vehicle bridge and cross over the South Fork of Middle Boulder Creek.

- Watch for trail marker to Lost Lake at about the 2.5-mile point.

- Avoid trails that go west. Continue south about 0.5 mile to the edge of Lost Lake.

- Return to the trailhead using the same route you came in on.

then bend to the west through a meadow before contouring east and ascending to the lake.

From the lake you should be able to see an abandoned mine on the craggy slopes of Bryan Mountain to the south. To the north you can view Chittenden Mountain. Lost Lake is a great spot to sit, relax, enjoy lunch, and take in the beauty of the Rocky Mountains. When you're ready to return home for the day, simply follow the same route you came in on back to the trailhead.

There are also three other trails in the area, all of which continue from the trail junction below Lost Lake: King Lake, Woodland Lake, and Devil's Thumb. All of these trails are more difficult than reaching Lost Lake. If you are a novice skier or snowshoer, you should not go farther or should go with an experienced backcountry traveler. In all three cases there are steep climbs and some avalanche danger; and the trail is not as heavily used, so you may need to break trail.

From the trail junction below Lost Lake, continue up the South Fork another 3.5 miles west to King Lake. Be careful on the last climb to the lake. The slope is steep and has some avalanche danger. Be sure to bring avalanche beacons and shovels if you plan to continue past Lost Lake.

Woodland Lake Trail leaves King Lake Trail at 0.2 mile past the junction to Lost Lake and continues along a wagon road north (right) up Jasper Creek. After 1 mile it turns left (west) from the Devil's Thumb Trail junction and climbs steeply, then levels off before reaching the lake.

Devil's Thumb Trail continues up the Jasper Creek drainage from the junction with Woodland Lake Trail. There is a steep section just after the junction that you will have to traverse. The road is difficult to find in this section. Both Devil's Thumb Lake and Jasper Lake are above the valley floor to the north. To find them climb toward the Devil's Thumb rock formation and then drop down to them once you have reached the head of the valley. It is 6.9 miles to Devil's Thumb Lake from the trailhead.

How to get there

From Boulder go west approximately 17 miles on Colorado Highway 119 to the town of Nederland. Go through the town and watch for signs to Eldora Mountain Resort. Make a right on County Road 130 and go through the town of Eldora. A little way past Eldora, the road will not be plowed and snow will block further travel. Park on the left side (south) and obey the NO PARKING signs.

Second Creek Cabin to Winter Park Resort

Berthoud Pass, Winter Park, CO

Type of trail:	
Also used by:	Downhill skiers at Winter Park Resort.
Distance:	3 miles to and from Second Creek Cabin; 5.5 miles one way from the trailhead to Winter Park Resort (shuttle required for return trip).
Terrain:	Gentle ascents and open areas for the first 2 miles, and then the more challenging climbs and descents to the end of trail at the resort.
Trail difficulty:	Intermediate to advanced.
Surface quality:	Ungroomed, but usually well tracked by skiers or snowshoers for the first 2 miles; then ungroomed backcountry conditions for rest of the trail.
Elevation:	The trail starts at 10,580 feet. Second Creek Cabin is at 11,200 feet, and the Winter Park Resort base is at 9,360 feet.
Time:	3 to 4 hours to the hut and back; 5 hours to all day from the trailhead to the resort.
Avalanche danger:	Low to moderate on the trail to Second Creek Cabin. There can be high avalanche danger in the bowls on the sides of the valleys.
Food and facilities:	Located less than two hours from downtown Denver, Berthoud Pass is popular with a lot of people for day skiing or snowshoeing. From Denver, convenience stores, gas stations, and restaurants are available all along I–70. A grocery store is located in Idaho Springs.

If you're planning on staying over, the closest full-service restaurants, ski shops, and overnight accommodations are found in the town of Winter Park. From Second Creek Campground and the trailhead, Winter Park is located a short 10 miles north on U.S. Highway 40. For information about hotels, motels, condos, and other facilities, call the Frasier Valley Chamber of Commerce at (800) 903–7275 or visit their Web site, www.winterpark-info.com.

For information about Second Creek Cabin, contact the Forest Service at (970) 887–4135. (Forest Service representatives say they are hopeful that the cabin will be re-opened for day use and overnight guests by the 2003–2004 winter season.)

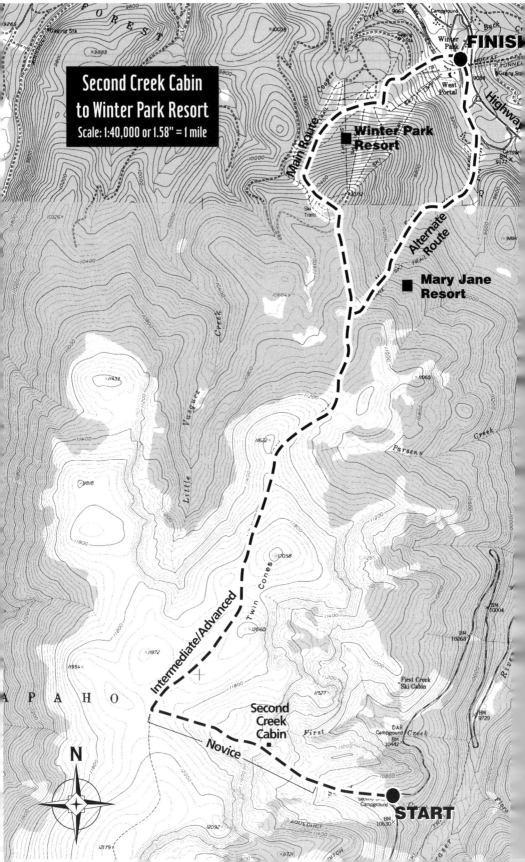

There are lots of reasons why Berthoud Pass is one of the most popular areas in the state for all types of winter sports. It's close to the Denver area. Skiers and snowshoers can combine backcountry adventures with a little downhill at Winter Park Resort. There is a variety of terrain available for cross-country touring, backcountry skiing, and snowshoeing.

The tour to Second Creek Cabin is short and scenic. Unfortunately Second Creek Cabin, also known as Gwen Andrews Hut, has fallen into disrepair in recent years, and the Forest Service has closed it. But planners at the Forest Service are working with a local association to replace the cabin and make it available for both day-use and overnight rental.

From the trailhead ski on the west side of the road, over the valley, staying on the north or on the right side of the creek. You'll start to climb through the trees; the path is generally well marked. Be sure to stay clear of the slopes on the south side of the valley because extreme avalanche danger may exist. Keep heading west and the trees thin out as you climb higher.

About halfway up the trail, you'll reach the steepest section on an open slope. Stay to the north as you climb and then, when the terrain flattens a bit, bend around to the south edge of the ridgeline.

You'll traverse a valley and follow the trail over another ridge, ascending north. At the top of the ridge, veer to the west and to the A-frame hut nestled by the trees. It's close to the ridge that divides First and Second Creeks.

If you want to extend your tour to First Creek Valley, head northwest for a little over 1 mile and connect with Mount Nystrom Trail. Veer northeast and follow the trail leading to the top of the main north-south ridge above First Creek Valley. Be careful of avalanche chutes on the southern side of the drainage. The trail starts out to the north and is pretty flat for the first 1 mile. After that it drops steeply and will lead you all the way to Winter Park Resort.

If you decide to make the entire tour, the route will fork about 3 miles down Mount Nystrom Trail. The path to the right leads you down the Mary Jane ski trail along Mary Jane Creek. It's about 1.75 miles down through some pretty steep drops to the road, which connects the bases of Winter Park and Mary Jane.

The trail that goes to the left has another 300-foot climb to the north; then it drops down to the top of the Winter Park ski area. It's a more gentle descent, but keep in mind that for the last 1 mile of downhill, you'll be on the ski slope with faster-moving downhill skiers.

Directions at a glance

- The trailhead begins at the parking area. Ski or snowshoe west over the valley, staying on the north or right side of the creek. The first 0.75 mile is relatively flat with gentle climbs. Stay clear of slopes on the south side of the valley because avalanche danger may exist.

- After 0.75 mile, the trail becomes steep for 0.1 mile as you traverse around the hill.

- At the 1-mile point, the trail flattens out and crosses the valley to the west and north.

- Look for Second Creek Hut across the valley.

- Return to the trailhead by the same route.

Alternate route

- From Second Creek Campground, take a shuttle vehicle and drive 6.5 miles north on U.S. Highway 40 to Winter Park Resort.

- Return to the Second Creek trailhead and follow the route to Second Creek Hut.

- Instead of turning around, intermediate or advanced skiers and snowshoers can traverse the open area above the hut going northwest from the hut and intersect with Mount Nystrom Trail.

- Turn right, heading north on Mount Nystrom Trail. Be cautious of avalanche chutes in the area.

- Mount Nystrom Trail is on relatively flat terrain for the first mile.

- The next 2 miles of the trail has steep ups and downs suited for advanced skiers and snowshoers.

- At just over 3 miles along Mount Nystrom Trail, the route forks.

- The trail to the right takes you down the Mary Jane ski trail for about 1.75 miles to the base area of Mary Jane.

- The trail to the left climbs steeply for a short distance and then descends down to the top of the ski lifts at Winter Park Resort.

- Both trails will take you to the base area at Winter Park Resort.

- Pick up your shuttle car and return to the Second Creek trailhead.

Tracks through an open glade.

Both trails end up at Winter Park Resort, which is a great place to relax and get something warm to drink and eat before picking up your shuttle car to shag the vehicle you left at the Second Creek trailhead.

How to get there

From Denver, head west on I–70 for approximately 42 miles to U.S. Highway 40. Take U.S. Highway 40 west approximately 15.5 miles to the top of Berthoud Pass—located between Empire and Winter Park. Three miles past the summit of Berthoud Pass, look for the turnout to the Second Creek trailhead. Parking can be found on the west side of the road. If you're planning on skiing or snowshoeing all the way to Winter Park Resort, you'll need to take your shuttle vehicle another 6.5 miles north on U.S. Highway 40 and park it in the lot at the ski resort.

Mount Bierstadt

Guanella Pass, Georgetown, CO

Type of trail:	━━ ⬯
Also used by:	Winter mountaineers.
Distance:	6.2 miles.
Terrain:	Steep and challenging climbs all the way to the summit.
Trail difficulty:	Advanced.
Surface quality:	Ungroomed and usually not well tracked by skiers or snow-shoers.
Elevation:	The trail starts at 11,650 feet and ends at the summit at 14,060 feet.
Time:	5 to 7 hours.
Avalanche danger:	Low to high, depending on conditions.
Snowmobile use:	Moderate traffic exists in flats of Scott Gomer Creek.
Food and facilities:	In and around the Guanella Pass area, there is little in the way of food or facilities. The closest moderate-sized town is Georgetown, 11 miles north on Guanella Pass Road. Hotels, motels, restaurants, and gas stations can be found in George-town. Contact the Georgetown Visitors Center at (303) 569–2888 for information about facilities in the area.

I f you want the experience of snowshoeing or cross-country skiing up one of Colorado's 14,000-foot peaks (known as fourteeners), the Guanella Pass route to Mount Bierstadt is one of the best. The route is steep in sections, the trail is difficult to follow, and the route is above treeline and exposed to the wind. But if the hardships don't scare you away, the view from the summit of one of the highest mountains in the state—overlooking the Front Range to the east and Keystone and Sum-mit County to the west—will make you think you can see forever!

During the summer months the many trails from Guanella Pass are loaded with hikers. During the winter the crowds clear out, and the route attracts skiers, snowshoers, and mountaineers. Be sure to check the avalanche conditions and make this tour only when the potential for slides is low. Just keep reminding yourself, as you ascend 2,400 feet in just over 3 miles, that for mountain climbers this is one of the easiest fourteeners. For cross-country skiers, think of the downhill ride on the way back!

From the trailhead and parking area, ski or snowshoe southeast across the flats about 0.75 mile to Scott Gomer Creek. Enjoy the descending

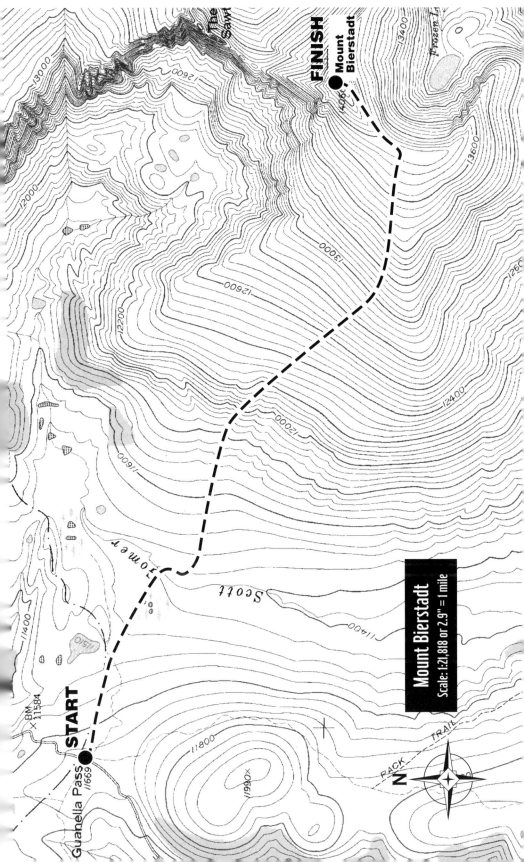

FINISH
Mount Bierstadt

The Sawt...

Frozen L...

13400

13000

13000

12600

12600

13000

13600

12000

13200

12800

12200

12000

12400

11600

13000

12600

Timel

Scott

11400

11400

Mount Bierstadt
Scale: 1:21,818 or 2.9" = 1 mile

11800

11800

11584
BM

START

Guanella Pass
11669

11810

11990

PACK

TRAIL

N

grade on this short stretch because after you cross the creek, it'll be uphill all the way to the summit. After crossing Scott Gomer Creek, angle your journey toward the headwall to the southeast. Be careful in these flats. The willows here are famous for being thick and difficult to cross even in the winter.

If you're lucky you'll be able to see tracks from skiers and snowshoers who have come through the area and broken the trail for you, but don't trust or expect this. Be sure to carry a topo map and a compass. Excellent navigating skills are a must on this advanced ski and snowshoe excursion because of strong winds and ground blizzards that may obstruct your ability to orient yourself.

At about the 1-mile point, start climbing the steep headwall above Scott Gomer Creek. Take a deep breath and tell yourself you're one-third of the way there. After the

Directions at a glance

- The trailhead at Guanella Pass begins at the parking area.
- Follow the trail southeast approximately 0.75-mile across Scott Gomer Creek.
- Head toward the "headwall" to the southeast. Begin climbing steeply up the headwall to the broad western ridge below the summit.
- Continue climbing southeast until reaching the southwest ridgeline.
- Follow the ridgeline for another 0.50 mile to the flat shoulder south of the summit.
- Head northeast along the top of the ridge to the summit of 14,060-foot Mount Bierstadt.
- Return to the trailhead by the same route and enjoy the steep descent.

steepest part of the climb up the headwall, continue climbing southeast until you reach the edge of the ridge where the slope drops away to the south. Turn east until you reach the flat shoulder to the right or south of the summit. Here turn left to the northeast and climb the top of the ridge to the summit at 14,060 feet.

Congratulations, you now have a fourteener to put in your logbook of adventures! For people who appreciate the real "Rocky Mountain high," that's a badge of high esteem. On your return down the mountain, the snow from the summit to the west ridge may not be the greatest. But from the ridgeline all the way down to the flats—and especially back down the headwall area—you're in for the thrill of your life.

Be careful to stay on the broad west ridge on the way down. In overcast, windy, or snowy conditions, it may be difficult to see the route. Use your compass to keep heading generally west-northwest from the shoulder below the summit to the top of Guanella Pass.

How to get there

Drive west from Denver on I–70 approximately 57 miles to exit 228 in Georgetown. Follow the main route through Georgetown to Guanella Pass Road, located at the southwest edge of town. Follow the winding road for approximately 11 miles (it'll become dirt) to the summit and park at the summit or slightly to the north.

Keystone Gulch

White River National Forest, Keystone, CO

Type of trail: ▬▬ 🌢

Also used by: Skiers and snowmobilers.

Distance: 10 miles to and from the bottom of the steep switchbacks; 5 miles up the switchbacks to the top of Wayback Lift and back.

Terrain: Moderately challenging climbs for beginners and then steep steps up to the top of the ski resort's lift.

Trail difficulty: Novice to intermediate.

Surface quality: Ungroomed, but sometimes tracked by skiers or snowshoers.

Elevation: The trail starts at about 9,200 feet and ends at 11,960 feet.

Time: 5 to 7 hours.

Avalanche danger: Low.

Snowmobile use: Only those belonging to Keystone Resort are allowed on the trail for maintenance.

Food and facilities: Located about 5 miles from the town of Dillon, Keystone Gulch Trail is close to facilities in Dillon or Silverthorne or at Keystone Resort. Hotels and motels in Dillon and Silverthorne provide moderately priced overnight accommodations. There are also grocery stores, convenience stores, gas stations, and a host of restaurants from fast food to complete sit-down facilities. For brochure information about the facilities in Dillon, contact the Summit County Chamber of Commerce at (800) 530–3099.

At Keystone Resort where Keystone Gulch Trail begins, you'll find several restaurants, cafeterias, and lounges, including two restaurants rated with four stars by AAA! You have a choice of five different hotels and inns located at the base of Keystone. The Keystone Cross-Country Center has a full line of equipment rentals and repairs. They also offer lessons and even moonlight tours. Information on lodging, guides, and tours can be obtained by calling (800) 427–8308 or (970) 496–4275.

The Keystone area has over 26 kilometers of groomed trails and an additional 50 kilometers of backcountry trails, mostly on old mining roads. Keystone Gulch Trail is a fun route because it runs up along-

START

Keystone Gulch
Scale: 1:34,286 or 1.85" = 1 mile

Santiago Lift

North Peak

FINISH

Wayback Lift

A R A P A H O

N A T I O N A L

N

Outback Express Lift

The Outback

turnaround for
novice skiers or snowshoers

A view from the top of Keystone.

side the southwest boundary of the ski area and is convenient for alpine skiers who want to try cross-country touring or snowshoeing for a different adventure. The only snowmobiles you'll see belong to employees of the resort who are using Keystone Gulch Road as a service road. The trail climbs gradually and only becomes too steep for the novice toward the end where it is recommended for intermediate and advanced skiers and snowshoers. Many skiers or snowshoers stop before the big ascent begins and head back about 5 miles from the trailhead.

If you want a vigorous workout, keep going up the switchback trail; it's the road that cuts left and heads steeply east, and it will take you another 2.5 miles to the top of the Wayback Lift. From there you can either go back down the road the way you came or head down on the ski lift trail to the bottom of Keystone Gulch. Do keep in mind that if you choose the latter route, you'll be sharing the terrain with fast-moving downhill skiers and snowboarders.

From the trailhead ski or snowshoe along Keystone Gulch Trail, which follows a four-wheel-drive road that heads south and then gently bends to the southeast. If you are a beginner, the first 5 miles are well suited to you because the trail climbs gradually through a heavily forested area and lacks hard turns. Although topographical maps should always be a part of your equipment, advanced map reading skills are not required here. Continue on the road, gaining more than 1,000 feet in elevation, but don't fret, you'll have 5 miles to get acclimated to the higher elevation. Rest whenever you need to.

The trail becomes more difficult after the first 5 miles where a wide switchback veers northeast and climbs steeply. If you are a novice, turn around at this point and head back downhill for a fun glide all the way to the trailhead. If you are an intermediate or advanced skier or snowshoer who wants a swift, fast climb, continue ascending more than 700 feet in just over 2 miles. Continue on the four-wheel-drive road to the east.

How to get there

From Denver take I–70 west approximately 70 miles to exit 205 to Dillon and Silverthorne. At the bottom of the off-ramp, make a left onto U.S. Highway 6. Go east through Dillon. U.S. Highway 6 will curve back around Dillon Reservoir to the south. Follow the signs to Keystone—U.S.

Directions at a glance

- Park in the plowed area off Keystone Gulch Road only! If no parking is available, park at Keystone Lodge and take the free shuttle bus to the trailhead.

- Head south on Keystone Gulch Trail and follow the old four-wheel-drive road.

- Climb gently uphill for approximately 5 miles along this road until it cuts to the east and begins a steep ascent.

- Turn back here and enjoy a gentle downhill glide or trek to the trailhead.

Alternate route

- At approximately 5 miles from the trailhead, the road cuts off to the left and heads steeply east.

- Continue to climb the 2.5 miles of switchbacks to the top of the Wayback Lift.

- Return to the trailhead by skiing or snowshoeing back down the switchback road and then through Keystone Gulch, or by going on one of the marked downhill ski runs.

- At the bottom of the ski run, turn left and head north back through Keystone Gulch to the trailhead.

Highway 6 then heads southeast and then east. Turn right at the traffic light marking the western entrance to Keystone Resort. Then make an immediate left and follow Keystone Road for 0.3 mile. At Soda Ridge Road turn right and follow it for 0.5 mile. Turn left onto Keystone Gulch Road (marked with a Keystone street sign) and go 0.1 mile to the winter closure gate. Park in the plowed area. If there is not enough parking available, park at Keystone Lodge and ride the free shuttle bus to the trailhead. If you're staying in Dillon, you can catch free, frequent shuttle buses from a variety of locations in town to Keystone and the trailhead. The Forest Service asks that you do not parallel park along Soda Ridge Road or park in any of the private drives.

Peru Creek

White River National Forest, Montezuma, CO

Type of trail:	▬▬ ⬭
Also used by:	Snowmobilers.
Distance:	8 miles.
Terrain:	Easy to moderately challenging climbs for the novice on the main trail. Steep ascents and descents for the advanced skier or snowshoer on the alternate route.
Trail difficulty:	Novice to advanced.
Surface quality:	Ungroomed, but often tracked by skiers or snowshoers.
Elevation:	The trailhead is at 10,030 feet and the trail climbs to 11,061 feet at the Pennsylvania Mine.
Time:	3 to 5 hours.
Avalanche danger:	Low on trail but increases at higher elevations.
Snowmobile use:	Low to moderate.
Food and facilities:	The Peru Creek trailhead is about 12.5 miles east of Dillon. Plan on staying in Dillon or at Keystone Resort. Information about lodging can be obtained from the Summit County Chamber of Commerce at (800) 530–3099. Or if you're planning on staying at Keystone Resort, call (800) 258–9553.
	Gas, groceries, water, and sack lunches should all be obtained before heading too far from Dillon or Keystone Resort. Once you get to the Peru Creek trailhead, there are no facilities.

If you are a novice skier or snowshoer who wants to take in the rich mining history of the area while enjoying a pleasant backcountry outing, the beginning part of this popular tour is well suited to you. Mine sites and remnants of old mining buildings whose stories are untold create a scenic foreground against the rugged mountains. In addition to a sack lunch and drinking water, taking your camera along is a must!

The Pennsylvania Mine, located at the end of this trail, was one of the better producers of silver ore in the area. Yielding high-quality silver ore, the mine was active from 1879 until the mid-1940s. If you are a more experienced skier or snowshoer, you may want to continue past the mine to Horseshoe Basin or scout around the areas of Chihuahua and Ruby Gulches to the north. Understand that you'll cross potentially dangerous avalanche chutes and must call the local avalanche hotline for the latest avalanche conditions. A complete list of avalanche hotlines is found in

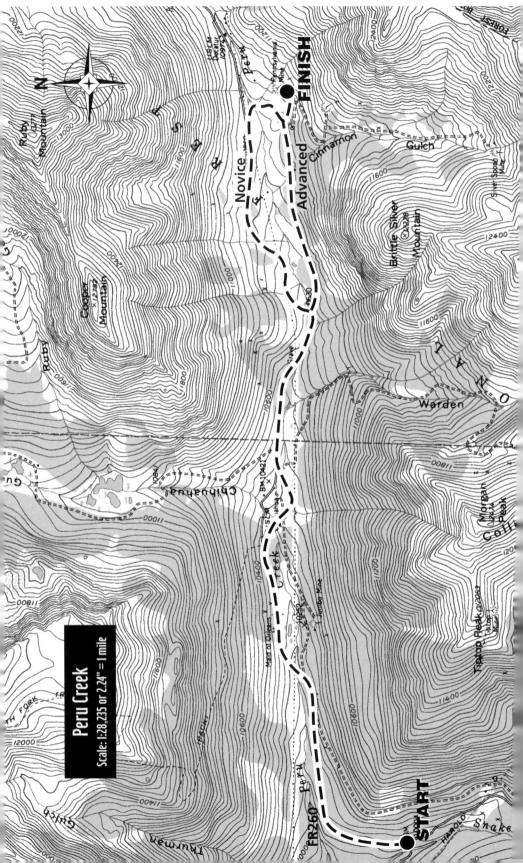

the appendix. Back in 1898, the town of Decatur—which is located right on the trail—was completely destroyed by an avalanche off of Grays Peak! If you plan to go past the Pennsylvania Mine, topo maps, avalanche beacons for everyone in the party, and snow shovels are highly recommended.

From the trailhead on Forest Road 260, start skiing or snowshoeing north through a wooded area along the roadbed as it bends around the hillside. After about 0.5 mile, the road will take you east into Peru Creek Valley. Right away Morgan Peak at 12,474 feet is in view on your right, and soon afterward the snow-capped 12,782-foot peak of Cooper Mountain can be seen to the east.

The trail continues to climb steadily for the first 1 mile. The trail forks, and the small trail heads off to the right. Stay on Forest Road 260 and veer toward the left. After 1.5 miles, you'll see the remnants of the old Maid of Orleans Mine to your left. Across the valley to the south of the trail is the Jumbo Mine. A little farther on you'll reach the mouth of Chihuahua Gulch.

The route starts to climb more vigorously, and by the 2-mile point you have already ascended 400 feet. The trail veers south for a bit and then heads east again, climbing another 200 feet in and out of the trees for the next 1 mile. At about 2.75 miles from the trailhead—about 1.25 miles past the Maid of Orleans Mine—watch carefully for an old tombstone on the left side of the trail. The stone is old and weathered, but it's a one-hundred-dred-year-old testament to many a miner who gave their lives seeking the riches of the Colorado mountains. After 3 miles, you'll cross to the south side of Peru Creek and see a fork in the road.

The best route for novice and intermediate skiers or snowshoers is to stay on Forest Road 260, which continues to the left toward Decatur. Go 1 mile and look for a trail that cuts off to the right and heads south. This is the easiest way to the Pennsylvania Mine. The mine's mill still stands today and makes for a picturesque background.

If you're an advanced skier or snowshoer and want to really challenge yourself with some steep climbs and descents, take the right fork and climb steeply along Brittle Silver Mountain. The route climbs steeply directly toward the mine and is not recommended for inexperienced skiers or snowshoers! Along this route after about the 4-mile mark, you'll pass Cinnamon Gulch and see the historic remnants of the Pennsylvania Mine.

Return to the trailhead along the same route and enjoy gentle glides or treks back down the 4-mile trail.

How to get there

From Denver go approximately 70 miles west on I–70 and take exit 205 to Dillon and Silverthorne. At the bottom of the off-ramp, turn left and head east on U.S. Highway 6 through the town of Dillon, then follow the

Directions at a glance

- The Peru Creek trailhead is marked Forest Road 260. Follow it north through an aspen grove and then east into Peru Creek Valley.
- The trail forks at 1 mile from the trailhead. Stay on Forest Road 260 and veer to the left.
- At the 1.5-mile marker, you'll see the old Maid of Orleans Mine.
- Go 1.25 miles past the Maid of Orleans Mine and look for the tombstone of a forgotten miner on the left side of the road.
- At about 3 miles from the trailhead, the route forks. For the easiest route veer left and stay on Forest Road 260.
- Go approximately 1 mile and look for the trail that cuts off to the right and heads south.
- Take the trail to the right about 0.25 mile and look to your left—you should be able to see the remnants of the abandoned Pennsylvania Mine and the mill that still stands today.
- To return, follow the same route back to the trailhead.

Alternate route

- At approximately 3 miles from the trailhead, the route splits. Forest Road 260 continues to the left.
- The trail to the right is suitable for advanced skiers and snowshoers only and includes lots of steep climbs and descents along Brittle Silver Mountain.
- The trail continues along the same path for approximately 1 mile and passes through Cinnamon Gulch.
- The trail ends about 0.25 mile below the old Pennsylvania Mine and the mill.
- To return, follow the same route back to the trailhead.

signs to Keystone. Stay on U.S. Highway 6 east, and approximately 1.6 miles past the intersection for Keystone Resort, which has a signal light, look for signs and a right-hand turn onto Montezuma Road (County Road 5). Continue on County Road 5 for 4.6 miles to the Peru Creek trailhead. It will be on your left and will be marked as Forest Road 260. The gate may be left open but please do not drive up this road. It is not passable. Park in the plowed area in front of the gate.

Saints John

White River National Forest, Montezuma, CO

Type of trail:	▬▬▬ ⬤
Also used by:	Snowmobilers.
Distance:	5.2 miles.
Terrain:	Short trail but steady and steep climbs.
Trail difficulty:	Novice to intermediate.
Surface quality:	Ungroomed, but often tracked by skiers or snowshoers.
Elevation:	Trail starts at 10,268 feet and ends at 11,500 feet.
Time:	3 to 5 hours.
Avalanche danger:	Moderate—trail lies in path of avalanche chutes.
Snowmobile use:	Moderate.
Food and facilities:	The town of Montezuma, where the Saints John trailhead can be found, is about 13.5 miles east of Dillon. Plan on staying in Dillon or at Keystone Resort. Information about lodging can be obtained from the Summit County Chamber of Commerce at (800) 530–3099. Or if you're planning on staying at Keystone Resort, call (800) 258–9553.
	Gas, groceries, water, and sack lunches should all be obtained before heading too far from Dillon or Keystone Resort. Once you get to Montezuma and the trailhead, there are no facilities.

This trail is ideal for history buffs who love to wander over roads used more than a hundred years ago by miners seeking their fortunes in silver. The Saints John Mine, which dates back to 1863, was the site of the first major silver strike in Colorado. This valley, formed by glaciers, once thrived, having a library, sawmill, mill, and smelter. But no saloons! The town was named after Saint John the Baptist and Saint John the Evangelist. The townsite was partially destroyed in the 1800s by an avalanche.

Most of the time the danger level is low on the trail up to the old ghost town of Saints John but can become moderate after that. If you are planning to go off the trail or beyond the Wild Irishman Mine, topo maps, avalanche beacons for everyone in the party, and snow shovels should be considered standard equipment.

The Saints John Trail is short but also steep, gaining 1,200 feet in just about 2.5 miles. It is definitely for the outdoorsperson in good physical shape. The end of the trail however rewards the hardy skier or snowshoer

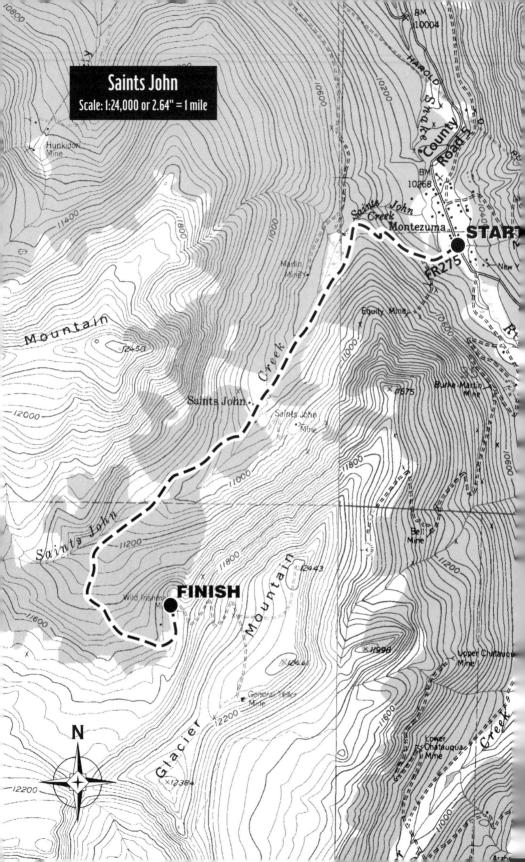

with spectacular views of two of Colorado's fourteeners: Grays Peak at 14,270 feet and Torreys Peak at 14,267 feet.

From the trailhead, which is marked as Forest Road 275, follow Saints John Road through the small town of Montezuma. Cross a bridge over the Snake River and begin climbing toward the northwest through a forest. On your left at approximately 0.25 mile from the trailhead, you'll see a small road leading to the site of the old Equity Mine. Stay on Forest Road 275 and continue northwest. The road makes a couple switchbacks as it climbs up a steep hill. Soon after you start your climb, you'll veer to the left or southwest, where you'll see the start of the Saints John Creek valley. Continue heading southwest, climbing steadily, and meandering into and out of the woods and meadows. After the trail crosses over the Saints John Creek, you'll spot several old buildings and a smelter chimney of the abandoned Saints John townsite. You've traveled about 1.2

Directions at a glance

- The Saints John trailhead is marked as Forest Road 275 and almost immediately there is a bridge crossing the Snake River.
- Head northwest on road through woods and past small road to left that leads to Equity Mine.
- Continue to climb and switchback to the northwest for another 0.5 mile.
- The trail bends to the southwest and starts up the Saints John Creek valley.
- Cross Saints John Creek at approximately the 1.2-mile mark, and you'll see the remnants and structures of the Saints John ghost town.
- Beginners can turn around here and go back on the same trail.

Alternate routes

- After reaching Saints John townsite, continue southwest on Forest Road 275.
- At the southwest edge of town, leave the road and stay close to the valley floor to avoid possible avalanche danger.
- After 0.5 mile climb back up and continue to follow the road.
- At approximately 2.5 miles from the trailhead, the trail turns south and climbs steeply to the Wild Irishman Mine and spectacular views of Grays Peak and Torreys Peak to the northeast.

Drifts above Saints John.

miles from Montezuma and the trailhead. A road off to the left leads to the actual mine. The buildings are privately owned and visitors are asked to stay away.

Though steep, the first half of the trail to Saints John is a well-traveled road suitable for novice cross-country skiers and snowshoers. The second half of the route climbs over more steep terrain and is better suited to intermediates. If you are a novice, the townsite offers plenty of good photo opportunities and is an ideal location to enjoy a fast glide or trek back to the trailhead after lunch.

If you're planning on pressing on for the view of Grays and Torreys Peaks, after leaving the townsite of Saints John, it's advised that you drop down from the road itself and follow Saints John Creek up the valley. This will help you to avoid a hazardous avalanche chute that's located just to the southwest of the town. After about 0.5 mile, you can return to the road and continue climbing southwest for another 0.5 mile. The route takes you into the woods and out into open meadows. At about the 2.5-mile point, the road turns to the left heading south and climbs more steeply until you're near treeline, then it veers to the north. The Wild Irishman Mine and indescribable views of two of Colorado's four-teeners are just up ahead.

How to get there

From Denver go approximately 70 miles west on I–70 and take exit 205 to Dillon and Silverthorne. At the bottom of the off-ramp, turn left and head east on U.S. Highway 6 through the town of Dillon, then follow the signs to Keystone. Stay on U.S. Highway 6 heading east, and approximately 1.6 miles past the intersection for Keystone Resort, marked by a signal light, look for signs and make a turn onto Montezuma Road (County Road 5). Continue on County Road 5 for 5.6 miles to the town of Montezuma. Park at the Saints John trailhead in the center of Montezuma.

Deer Creek

White River National Forest, Montezuma, CO

Type of trail:	▬▬▬ ▦
Also used by:	Snowmobilers.
Distance:	5.2 miles.
Terrain:	Nice slow and gentle climbs to end of the trail.
Trail difficulty:	Novice.
Surface quality:	Ungroomed, but often tracked by skiers and snowshoers.
Elevation:	The trail starts at 10,500 feet and ends at 11,400 feet.
Time:	3 to 4 hours.
Avalanche danger:	Low.
Food and facilities:	Montezuma, where the trailhead to Deer Creek is, can be found 13.5 miles east of Dillon. Plan on staying in Dillon or Silverthorne or at Keystone Resort. Information about lodging can be obtained from the Summit County Chamber of Commerce at (800) 530–3099. Or if you're planning on staying at Keystone Resort, call them at (800) 258–9553.
	Gas, groceries, water, and sack lunches should all be obtained before heading too far from Dillon or Keystone Resort. Once you get to the townsite of Montezuma and then onto the Deer Creek trailhead, there are no facilities.

The Deer Creek Trail is a short, easy route for novice nordic skiers or snowshoers who don't want the crowds they may encounter at the Saints John or Peru Creek Trails. Located at the end of Montezuma Road, the trail gets less use than the popular routes found throughout the area. If you want to be alone in the backcountry, Deer Creek is the answer. Laced with remnants of once bountiful silver mines, the trail offers much to look at in terms of mining history, and the four-wheel-drive road it follows is usually well tracked. Don't choose a windy day, though. Even though the tour is below treeline, the large, open clearings and meadows can make for a blustery outing.

From the end of the plowed road, the trail heads south immediately. Ignore the side roads that veer off to the east and west. Soon after getting on the trail, County Road 5 becomes Forest Road 5. Once past the old sawmill on your left, you'll begin to see evidence of the area's rich mining history with the Superior Mine to the west, the first of many along the route. A road goes to the mine from the west, but you should avoid it. A lot of the mines, though inactive, are still privately owned, and you're asked to respect the rights of property owners.

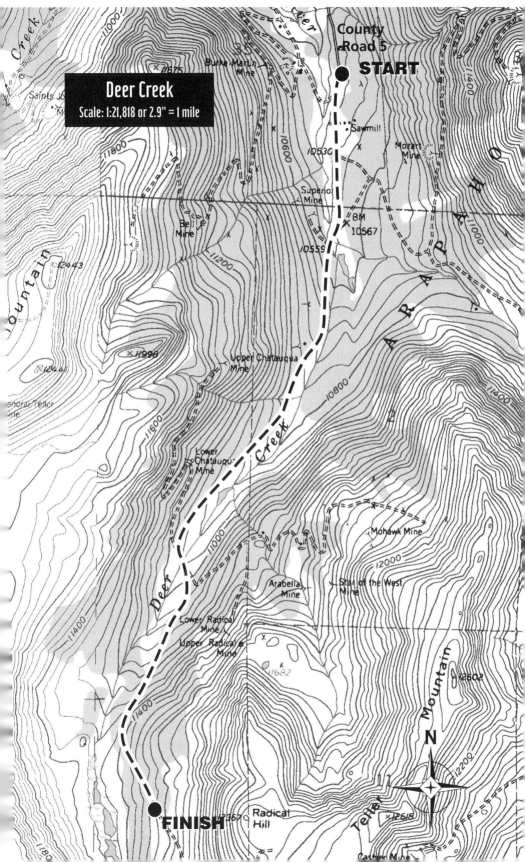

Continue south on Forest Road 5, which parallels Deer Creek, into a clearing and then back into the woods. You'll pass Upper Chatauqua Mine after 1 mile and Lower Chatauqua Mine 0.5 mile later. After beginning to climb steadily you'll see Star of the West Mine, Arabella Mine, Mohawk Mine, and Upper and Lower Radical Mines to the east.

Continuing on Forest Road 5 you'll meander into the trees and then out into clearings, climbing a little before the trail levels off. At about the 3-mile point when you're near treeline, you'll see the steep grades of the slopes to Radical Hill to your right and east. Although it's called Radical Hill, it's really a mountain with an elevation of 12,367 feet. To the west is Glacier Mountain, which towers to a height of 12,441 feet. Sculpted by forceful winds, these massive cornices take your breath away.

If you are a beginning skier or snowshoer, this is the spot to turn around. To return to the trailhead, just go back the way you came and enjoy the slight downhill grade.

How to get there

From Denver go approximately 70 miles west on I–70 and take exit 205 to Dillon and Silverthorne. At the bottom of the off-ramp, turn left and head east on U.S. Highway 6. Go through the town of Dillon, and follow signs to Keystone. Stay on U.S. Highway 6 east, and approximately 1.6 miles past the first intersection to Keystone Resort, look for signs and turn right onto Montezuma Road (County Road 5). Continue on County Road 5 for 5.6 miles to the town of Montezuma. Park at the Saints John trailhead in the center of Montezuma. Or if the road is open, continue through Montezuma to the end of the road.

Directions at a glance

- Depending on where the snow closure area is, the Deer Creek trailhead begins at the end of the plowed road and heads south. Look for trail signs for Forest Road 5.

- Pass the sawmill on your left or east side, and you'll start to see remnants and structures of old abandoned mines.

- The trail continues to follow Forest Road 5 along Deer Creek with gentle climbs.

- At about the 3-mile point, the trail begins to climb steeply. For the novice skier or snowshoer, it's time to turn around and enjoy the gentle downhill trip back to the trailhead.

Mesa Cortina

White River National Forest, Dillon, CO

Type of trail:	▬▬ 👣
Distance:	7 miles.
Terrain:	Gentle climbs and gradual ascents.
Trail difficulty:	Novice to intermediate.
Surface quality:	Ungroomed, but sometimes tracked by skiers and snowshoers.
Elevation:	The trail starts at 9,200 feet and ends at 9,560 feet.
Time:	3 to 5 hours.
Avalanche danger:	The first 3.5 miles are low; after that and at the higher elevations, extreme avalanche danger exists.
Food and facilities:	This trail is located just outside the city limits of Silverthorne. There are plenty of hotels, motels, grocery stores, convenience stores, and fast-food outlets less than ten minutes from the trailhead. Because the trail goes into the Eagles Nest Wilderness Area, there are no facilities found on the trail itself. Pack in your lunches, drinks, etc.—and pack out your trash!
	If you want to stay in the area overnight, call the Summit County Chamber of Commerce at (800) 530–3099, or visit their Web site, www.summitchamber.com.

The Mesa Cortina Trail is an excellent choice for beginners because the route follows terrain that climbs gently. Overall elevation change from the trailhead to the turnaround point is less than 360 vertical feet over 3.5 miles. What can make this route tricky is that it's not well marked, and after a fresh snowfall, when you have to break the trail, it can be difficult to follow. Carrying a good set of topographic maps of the area should be considered a must. The open meadows, sloping away to the Blue River Valley and the trek through parts of the Eagles Nest Wilderness Area, make this a unique outdoor experience. Views of Silverthorne and Ptarmigan Mountains add to the splendor.

From the trailhead ski north through groves of aspen and meadows dotted with sagebrush. You'll peek out over the Blue River Valley and continue on, bending around to the northwest. At the edge of a lodgepole pine forest, you'll officially enter the Eagles Nest Wilderness Area. Skiing north and then veering to the northwest, you'll go down a hill and see a trail come in from the east a little over 2 miles from the trailhead. A short distance ahead is South Willow Creek, a good spot to relax and

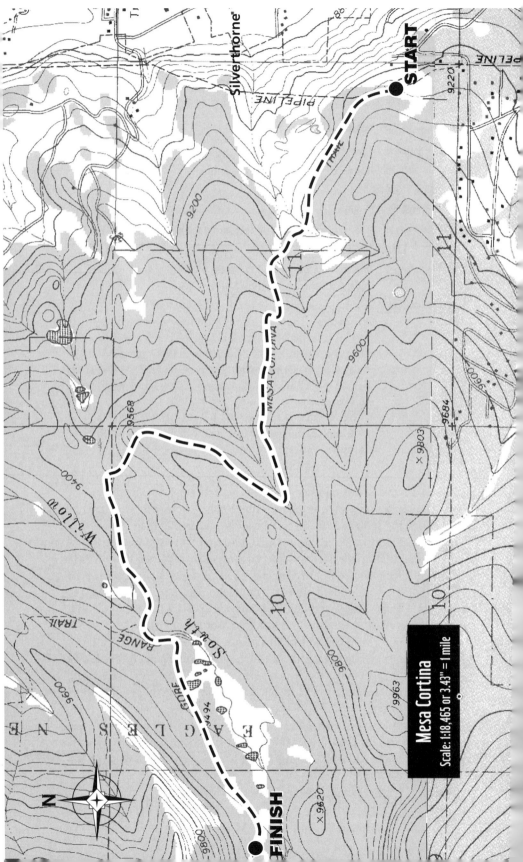

Heading up South Willow Creek from Mesa Cortina.

breathe in the scent of the pines. The creek originates behind Buffalo Mountain to the southwest, rushing down between the Buffalo's mighty 12,777-foot peak and Red Mountain's 13,189-foot pinnacle.

Cross over the creek. Here the trail joins with the Wheeler–Gore Range Trail. Take the trail that goes to your left, and for 1 mile you'll ski or snowshoe up a hill to the upper end of an open meadow. The trail basically follows the route of South Willow Creek. At 9,560 feet, this meadow makes for a fun picnicking spot and turnaround area.

Beyond this meadow is a steep climb over a large cliff scraped down by the glacier that formed the valley. This is a difficult trail and is not recommended for novice skiers or snowshoers.

How to get there

From I–70 take exit 205 to Dillon and Silverthorne. Turn right onto Colorado Highway 9, then turn left onto Wildernest Road at the first intersection past the highway interchange. (Wendy's restaurant will be on your right.) Take Wildernest Road for 0.2 mile, then turn right onto Adams Avenue. Almost immediately turn left onto Royal Buffalo Mountain Road (County Road 1240). Go 0.8 mile on Royal Buffalo Road and take a sharp right onto Lakeview Drive. Proceed 0.5 mile and turn left onto Aspen Drive. Travel a short distance to a parking area on the left and the trailhead on your right.

Directions at a glance

- The trailhead is on the right side of Aspen Drive.

- Take the trail north and northwest through groves of trees for approximately 2 miles.

- Here the trail will intersect a jeep trail coming in from the east.

- Stay on the trail to the northwest until crossing South Willow Creek.

- Across the creek Mesa Cortina Trail intersects with the Wheeler–Gore Trail.

- Go left on Wheeler–Gore Trail along South Willow Creek for approximately 1 mile.

- Rest here before turning around. Do not go into the dangerous avalanche area beyond.

- Return to the trailhead via the same route, and you'll enjoy gentle downhill trekking or skiing.

Lily Pad Lake

White River National Forest, Silverthorne, CO

Type of trail:	═══ ▱
Distance:	3 miles.
Terrain:	Gentle grades and lots of flat open forest areas.
Trail difficulty:	Novice.
Surface quality:	Ungroomed, but usually tracked by skiers or snowshoers.
Elevation:	The trail starts at about 9,500 to 9,600 feet.
Time:	1 to 3 hours.
Avalanche danger:	Low.
Food and facilities:	There's a good selection of hotels, motels, and restaurants in Dillon, Silverthorne, and Frisco. Information on restaurants and accommodations can be obtained by calling the Summit County Chamber of Commerce at (800) 530–3099 or visit their Web site at www.summitchamber.com.
	Gas, groceries, and drinks can also be found nearby, and it's recommended that you stock up before leaving. You won't find facilities or food near Lily Pad Lake Trail.

This is a popular trail for nordic skiers and snowshoers in the Dillon and Silverthorne area. Because it enters the Eagles Nest Wilderness Area, no mechanized vehicles or snowmobiles are allowed there. Ideal for beginners, the trail is pleasant for even the most inexperienced skier and snowshoer. Lily Pad Lake Trail is short, has the gentlest of grades, and meanders through meadows and in and out of stands of spruce and aspen to wind up at the pristine, frozen lake. Lily Pad Lake is ideal for picnicking and picture taking.

Surrounded by beaver ponds, the area was a favorite of fur trappers in the early 1800s. Gold was reported to the north in the Salt Lick Gulch area by a pioneer who told everyone that he had found "gold dust" in the mouth of a deer he had just shot for food. When the word got around, hordes of miners arrived, and the Salt Lick Gulch area became an important mining center. Like so many of the reported "get-rich-quick" mining areas, those who came and mined the Salt Lick went home licking their financial wounds.

Today the area is a novice skier and snowshoer's paradise. From the Lily Pad trailhead, you'll start at the top of the Wildernest subdivision. You'll encounter a climb to the water tank that services the homes, and if you are a novice skier, you might find it intimidating. If you are a

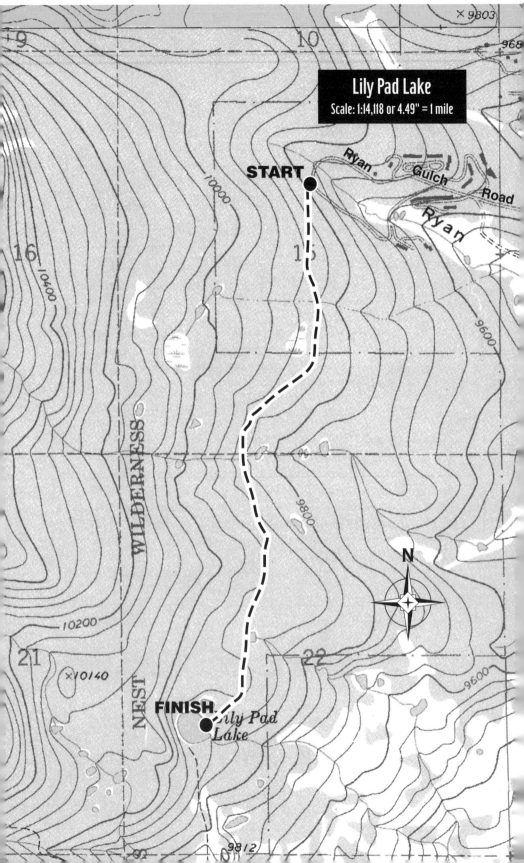

A view along Lily Pad Lake Trail.

beginner, don't worry. Take it easy and realize that once you're on top, the rest of the trail is a breeze!

After cresting the first big hill, go past the water reservoirs on the left and into the lodgepole forest. The trail turns north and then west. Each leg is only about 0.13 of a mile. At about 0.75 mile from the trailhead, look for another trail that intersects Lily Pad Lake Trail from your left. Take the trail to the right. Another 0.75 mile of gentle ascent and you'll arrive at Lily Pad Lake.

How to get there

From Denver take I–70 west approximately 70 miles to exit 205 (Dillon and Silverthorne). Go north on Colorado Highway 9. Turn left at the first light past the highway interchange onto Ryan

Directions at a glance

- Look for a ROAD CLOSED sign and a wire cable at the trailhead to Lily Pad Lake.

- Go west on the trail and plan for a steep climb during the first 0.25 to 0.5 mile.

- The trail levels out to nearly flat ground on top.

- At about 0.75 mile, look for signage to Lily Pad Lake. The trail will cut off to your right and go another 0.75 mile to the lake.

- Return to the trailhead by following the same trail back down and enjoy the gentle downhill glide or trek.

Gulch Road, and continue past Wildernest Hospitality Center. Follow this road almost 3 miles until it begins to go downhill. This is the farthest end of a large loop. Park at the end of the loop, and go to the ROAD CLOSED sign and wire cable at the southern end of the parking area. Look for the big water tank on the hill in front of you. Lily Pad Lake Trail begins here.

North Tenmile Creek

White River National Forest, Frisco, CO

Type of trail:	▬▬ ⬤
Also used by:	Snowmobilers for the first 2.5 miles.
Distance:	10 miles.
Terrain:	Steep climb at the beginning and then gentle to moderate climbs to the trail's end.
Trail difficulty:	Intermediate.
Surface quality:	Ungroomed, but usually well tracked by skiers or snowshoers.
Elevation:	The trailhead is at 9,400 feet, and you will climb to 10,250 feet at the trail's end.
Time:	5 hours to full day.
Avalanche danger:	Low.
Snowmobile use:	Moderate.
Food and facilities:	There's a good selection of hotels, motels, and restaurants in the town of Frisco. The closest overnight accommodations to North Tenmile Creek Trail are in Frisco. For information on restaurants and accommodations, call the Summit County Chamber of Commerce at (800) 530–3099.
	Gas, groceries, sack lunches, and drinks can also be found in Frisco. Stock up before leaving town. You won't find facilities or food near North Tenmile Creek.

North Tenmile Creek is a good choice for a tour because no motorized vehicles are allowed in the Eagles Nest Wilderness Area. You're then alone with canyons carved thousands of years ago by glaciers and the towering snow-capped peaks of Wichita Mountain, at 10,855 feet, and Chief Mountain, at 10,880 feet.

From the trailhead, head west. The first 0.5 mile of the trail is somewhat intimidating and exhilarating because of a steep climb up into the trees. If you are snowshoeing, definitely plan on carrying ski poles; if you are skiing, you should have "skins" for the steep ascent.

Once you've made the big push, the ground levels off to a gradual climb. For the next 2 miles or so, you'll glide or trek past numerous beaver ponds, wood thickets, and the remnants of old mines. In the early part of the century, miners used this trail to cart out thousands of pounds of gold and silver ore. Snow-covered tailing mounds can be seen dotting the landscape.

Continue through meadows and past another pond, and then you'll meander in and out of glades of aspen and pine. At about the 2.5-mile

Directions at a glance

- The trailhead for North Tenmile Creek begins at the west end of the parking area. Follow the trail heading steeply uphill to the west.

- After the first 0.5 mile, the trail levels out and continues to climb gently for the next 2-plus miles.

- At approximately 2.5 miles, you'll enter the Eagles Nest Wilderness Area.

- At about 3.5 miles from the trailhead, look for the intersection with the Gore Range Trail, which runs north to south.

- This is a good point to turn around and go back, otherwise it's another 1.5 miles up the trail to the northwest. Steep mountains border the trail to the west.

- To return to the trailhead, follow the same trail back to the trailhead.

point, you'll enter the Eagles Nest Wilderness Area, home to snowshoe hares, fox, coyotes, and other winter wildlife. Look for Forest Service's wooden signs that are posted at this point. They'll tell you that you are entering a designated wilderness area, and it's at this point that no mechanized vehicles are allowed. Red-tailed hawks and golden eagles return to this area to spend the warmer late-winter and early-spring months. And even though the snows are still deep on the ground, these residents come home to roost and provide some great photo opportunities.

The trail takes you past several clearings, and you'll continue west through more forest. At about the 3.5-mile point, you'll come to the junction of the Gore Range Trail. Snowshoeing and skiing opportunities abound by going left or right, but to complete this trail you'll need to keep going west on North Tenmile Creek Trail and enjoy the gentle ascent that will lead you into a flat and open valley. Views of the Gore Range Mountains are ahead, and they are magnificent. You may wish to use this as a resting area and turn back. However, if you want to go on, you'll see that the trail contours northwest until the valley ends beside steep snowy slopes. For the return trip, just head east on the trail and enjoy the downhill. The trip should go fast. And remember the last 0.5 mile to the trailhead that was such a steep climb at the beginning will now be a challenging downhill descent.

How to get there

From Denver take I–70 west approximately 75 miles to exit 201 (Frisco Main Street). Immediately after exiting the freeway, turn right into a plowed parking area. The trailhead is located immediately off the interstate exit on the north side.

Shrine Pass

White River National Forest, Vail Pass, CO

Type of trail:	═══ ⬭
Also used by:	Snowmobilers.
Distance:	5.1 miles to and from Shrine Pass, 6 miles to and from the Shrine Mountain Inn, and 11 miles one way to Red Cliff.
Terrain:	Gentle grades and lots of flat open forest areas.
Trail difficulty:	Novice to intermediate.
Surface quality:	Ungroomed, but usually tracked by skiers and snowshoers. The road to Red Cliff is often heavily used by snowmobiles.
Elevation:	The trail begins at 10,580 feet and ends at the town of Red Cliff at 8,680 feet.
Time:	3 to 5 hours to the pass and the cabins; all day to Red Cliff.
Avalanche danger:	Low.
Snowmobile use:	Moderate to heavy.
Food and facilities:	Vail is only 10 miles to the west. It's a great place to play and stay, offering luxury hotels, bed-and-breakfasts, and condominiums. For information on lodging, call Vail/Beaver Creek Central Reservations (800–525–2257). Make sure you get your groceries, sack lunches, and drinks before leaving Vail. Food is not available once you get up onto Vail Pass.
	The Shrine Mountain Inn consists of three cabins—Jay's, Chuck's, and Walter's. Each can accommodate up to twelve overnight guests. Chuck's and Walter's Cabins are split into upstairs and downstairs units and must be rented by single parties. The Shrine Mountain Inn is operated by the 10th Mountain Division Hut Association. Cabin information and reservations can be obtained by calling (303) 925–5775.

Unlike most other areas found throughout Colorado that are open and free to the public for skiing and snowshoeing, Vail Pass is now part of a "fee demonstration area." You will have to pay a user fee, and the money collected will be used to manage this heavy-use area. Self-fee tubes are available at all access points to the area. For information about the fees, call the Holy Cross ranger district office at (970) 827–5715. If you are planning to ski to Red Cliff, consider shuttling a car to the end of the trail. Getting to Red Cliff is relatively easy, but coming back is a long uphill climb.

Shrine Pass Trail is named for its spectacular views of the snow-

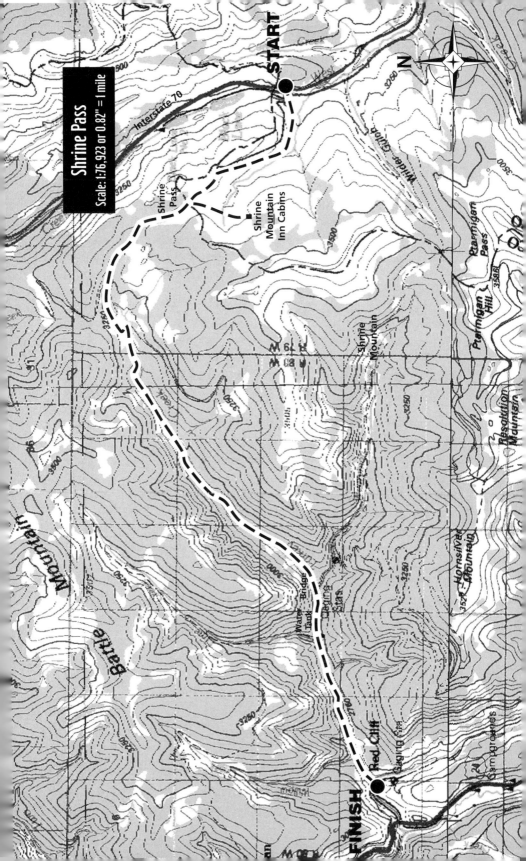

covered cross emblazoned on the side of the mountain, Mount of the Holy Cross, immortalized in writings by Ralph Waldo Emerson. The trail has many attractions: It mostly follows a wide and heavily used dirt road and a creek so you don't need advanced map-reading skills. It has 9 miles of downhill and so goes relatively quickly. And it's so popular that it is usually tracked by skiers and snowmobiles. If you are a novice skier or snowshoer, you may be able to stretch yourself with a longer journey, but not necessarily a more difficult one. The first 2 miles offer a workout with moderate uphill climbs. The rest of the journey is pleasantly downhill. Do however be aware that the trail is also very popular with snowmobilers and so care must be taken to stay out of each other's way.

Because of the snowmobile traffic, the surface of the road is adequate for skate skiing and affords a novel trip for skate skiers who want to journey outside a nordic center.

Although separate from the snowmobile trail, which follows Shrine Pass Road to the top of the pass, the cross-country ski and snowshoe trail begins at the same place near the entrance to the rest area at the begin-

Directions at a glance

- The trailhead begins at the parking lot (pay your day-use fee!) and climbs steadily below and to the left of Shrine Pass Road.
- At just over 2.5 miles from the trailhead, you'll reach the top of Shrine Pass.
- At about 2.7 miles from the trailhead, the road to the left will lead you to the Shrine Mountain Inn.
- If going to the cabins, take the trail to the left and go 0.3 mile.
- Return to the trailhead by going back by the same route.

Alternate route

- If you're not planning on going to the Shrine Mountain Inn and want to continue on to the town of Red Cliff, stay on Shrine Pass Road.
- Approximately 0.5 mile up from the cutoff to the cabins, you'll be able to see Mount of the Holy Cross. Watch for the signs and the overlook.
- Continue on the road along the north side of Turkey Creek.
- The trail ends in the small town of Red Cliff.
- To return to the trailhead, it's 11 miles back on the same route. Or pick up the shuttle vehicle you left.

Chuck's Cabin at the Shrine Mountain Inn.

ning of Shrine Pass Road. Staying well below and to the left of the road, the trail is well marked and climbs steadily but not too steeply to the west. After 1 mile it swings slowly to the northwest until it joins the snowmobile trail at the top of the pass, 2.5 miles from the trailhead. The route stays mostly on the right side of the valley overlooking the open parks in the valley below.

Once you cross the summit, you have a myriad of options. If you've had enough of a journey and don't want to spend all day on the trail, you can head back to the trailhead the way you came. Or you can go left, heading southwest for 0.3 mile along a well-traversed road into glades of trees to the Shrine Mountain Inn. Privately owned, the inn is a part of the 10th Mountain Division Hut Association and is a fun place for an overnight—or longer—stay. There are vast areas of deep powder here where you can have fun in the backcountry. The inn itself is made up of three cabins: Jay's, Chuck's, and Walter's. Reservations are necessary. The cost for staying overnight in Jay's Cabin and downstairs in Walter's Cabin is $35 per person. The upstairs units of Chuck's and Walter's Cabins must be rented as a unit for $210. Each sleeps six. That's a little more expensive than most of the other cabins, huts, and yurts throughout Colorado, but these fancy cabins are complete with running water, showers, electricity, and a sauna. The downstairs unit of Chuck's Cabin costs $25 per person. If you're planning on stopping off at the cabins for day use, you'll find that there is an additional day-use fee. You can make reservations through the 10th Mountain Division Hut Association (303–925–5775).

If you're not going to the Shrine Mountain Inn and plan on continuing to Red Cliff, keep on Shrine Pass Road, heading northwest. The descent will start at the head of the Turkey Creek drainage where the valley curves to the west. At the 3.25-mile point you can rest and enjoy the endless vistas of Mount of the Holy Cross at an overlook.

Continuing on the road, you'll ski along the north side of Turkey Creek, around open meadows, and then in and out of the woods, descending gradually. Over the next several miles, you'll cross over Turkey Creek and pass a bridge to Wearyman Creek and a water tank before you eventually enter the town of Red Cliff. The trail ends almost at the back door of a small restaurant in Red Cliff. It's a good spot to have a cup of coffee or a bite to eat before reversing your route or getting in the car.

How to get there

From Denver go west on I–70 approximately 90 miles to exit 190 at Vail Pass. If you're coming from Vail, take I–70 east for about 10 miles to exit 190 at Vail Pass. Immediately after getting off the freeway, you'll see a large parking lot on the west side of the interstate. It's kept plowed all winter, and it has a rest stop and a warming hut.

To shuttle a car to Red Cliff, take I–70 to exit 171 and turn right off the ramp onto U.S. Highway 24. Drive 10.2 miles through the town of Minturn and the abandoned town of Gilman. Turn left onto Forest Road 709 and drive about a mile to Red Cliff.

Commando Run

White River National Forest, Vail Pass, CO

Type of trail:	▬▬▬
Also used by:	Snowmobilers for first 4 miles; downhill skiers for the last 2 miles at Vail Resort.
Distance:	18 miles (one way only trail; leave shuttle vehicle in Vail).
Terrain:	Challenging steep climbs and descents.
Trail difficulty:	Advanced.
Surface quality:	Ungroomed backcountry and usually well tracked by skiers.
Elevation:	The Vail Pass trailhead is at 10,580 feet; Vail Resort is at 8,331 feet.
Time:	One full day.
Avalanche danger:	Moderate.
Snowmobile use:	Moderate to heavy for first 4 miles, then none.
Food and facilities:	Vail, only 10 miles west of Vail Pass, is a great place to play and stay. Luxury hotels, bed-and-breakfasts, and condominiums are available. For information on the more than sixty different lodging options, call Vail/Beaver Creek Central Reservations (800–525–2257). Make sure you get your groceries and drinks before leaving Vail. There's no place to buy food once you get to Vail Pass. Ski rentals and repairs can be taken care of at the Nordic Center, located at the Vail Golf Course Clubhouse (970–845–5313). Guides for the Commando Run are also available through the Vail Nordic Center.

The Commando Run from Vail Pass back to Vail Resort is regarded as one of the most challenging and best ski tours in Colorado. The Commando Run is named for the U.S. Army's 10th Mountain Division soldiers who used to train along this demanding route for high-altitude skiing combat and the commando raids during World War II. Popular today for its outstanding views and quality of snow, it's often tracked and can be accomplished in one full, hardy day of skiing. As with all winter activities at the top of Vail Pass, skiing the Commando Run requires paying a day-use fee.

The Commando Run gets its advanced rating for several reasons. The tour is long and the terrain is difficult. Map-reading and compass skills are a must. Even though many parts of the route are well defined, skiers will encounter sections along ridgelines that are not marked, where it's easy to go off in the wrong direction. If you are an experienced backcountry skier, however, the tour is an enjoyable test of stamina and technique. If you're not sure you want to tackle the Commando Run without a little help, you

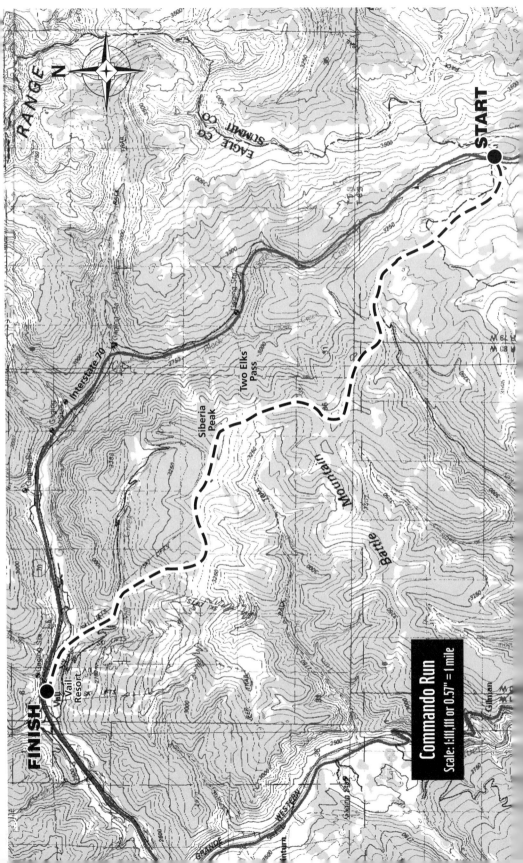

Commando Run
Scale: 1:111,111 or 0.57" = 1 mile

may want to consider arranging for a guide through the Vail Nordic Center (970–845–5313).

Start at the Vail Pass cross-country trailhead, across the rest area access road from the upper parking lot. The cross-country ski trail is separate from the main Shrine Pass Road, which is reserved for snowmobiles. The route is well marked with trail signs and contours across the slopes to the left and below Shrine Pass Road. To the left is the large meadow that curves down from the top of the pass. After 1 mile the trail swings to the right until it intersects with the snowmobile trail at the top of Shrine Pass.

Continue on Shrine Pass Road northwest and start descending at the head of the Turkey Creek drainage where the valley curves to the west. Pass the Mount of the Holy Cross overlook, skiing on the north side of Turkey Creek. At about the 4-mile point, the trail intersects Timber Creek Road (designated Forest Road 712) at a left-hand bend in the road. Take this road to the right, or north, climbing for 0.5 mile to the northwest. Soon this road forks and you should take Lime Creek Road, which veers to the left or west.

About 0.25 mile beyond the fork, look for the trail that leaves the road to the right. There is a sign that says TWO ELKS PASS 4 MILES. Entering the woods you'll start to climb steeply bearing to the left. The trail should follow the contour around to the southwest side of the hill and then to the top of the ridge. Continue west once on top of the ridge. At about the 6-mile point, contour north, climbing again to another elevation point of 11,710 feet. Take a breather and look out over the endless views of the Gore Range Mountains to the north.

Ski along the top of the ridge northwest to a sign for Bowman's Shortcut. Here head northeast and stay high on the ridge for 0.5 mile or so before contouring to the left of the ridge. When the contour shifts to the right, descend the wide ridge to Two Elks Pass. Just to the northwest you can see China Bowl and the Back Bowls of Vail. Climb north over the open, often windy south face of Siberia Peak, elevation 11,816 feet, and follow the ridge to the top of the Orient Express chair lift. Descend the ridge to Two Elks Lodge, a large wooden beam building on the ridge. Ski down the front side of Vail by taking Boomer to the bottom of the Sourdough lift (Chair 14) then following Northwoods to the bottom of Northwoods Express (Chair 11). From here take the North Face catwalk to Prima and down to Brisk Walk Road. This will take you to Golden Peak, where you can ski to the bottom of either Golden Peak or the bottom of Vista Bahn chair lift and the top of Bridge Street in Vail. This route combines both novice and intermediate level ski slopes to the bottom of the mountain.

How to get there

From Denver take I–70 west approximately 90 miles to exit 190 at Vail Pass. From Vail take I–70 east for 10 miles and get off at exit 190. There is a large parking lot west of the interstate that is plowed all winter and has a rest stop and a warming hut. (There's a day-use fee. Please pay it.) Since it's one-way from Vail Pass down to Vail Resort, make sure that you leave a shuttle car at the base of the ski resort.

Unlike most other areas found throughout Colorado that are open and free to the public for skiing and snowshoeing, Vail Pass is now part of a "fee demonstration area." You will have to pay a user fee. The money collected will be used to manage this heavy-use area. Self-fee tubes are available at all access points to the area. For information about the fees, call the Holy Cross National Forest district office at (970) 827–5715.

Directions at a glance

- The trailhead begins at the parking lot and climbs gently for first 2 miles, contouring above the meadows and below Shrine Pass Road.
- At 2.5 miles the cross-country trail intersects with Shrine Pass Road at the top of the pass.
- At about 2.7 miles from the trailhead, the road to the left cuts off to the Shrine Mountain Inn.
- Approximately 0.5 mile up from the cutoff to the cabins, you'll be able to see Mount of the Holy Cross. Watch for the signs and the overlook.
- Continue on the trail and you'll ski or snowshoe along the north side of Turkey Creek.
- At about the 4-mile point, the trail intersects with Timber Creek Road (Forest Road 712).
- Take Timber Creek Road to the right, then climb for 0.5 mile north and northwest.
- When Timber Creek Road forks, take the route to the left (Lime Creek Road) and head west.
- Two Elks Trail leaves and climbs bearing left to the ridge.
- At the top follow the ridge across a forested flat saddle and then up a short steep hill until coming out in a broad high meadow.
- Bowman's Shortcut. Follow the trail northeast into the woods and stay high on the ridge until bearing left along the contour of the hill.
- Descend to the top of China Bowl at Two Elks Pass.
- Continue north climbing Siberia Peak, then follow the ridge to the Orient Express chair lift.
- Descend Vail Resort to the Vista Bahn chair lift.

Corral Creek

White River National Forest, Vail Pass, CO

Type of trail:	▬▬ 🔄
Also used by:	Snowmobilers.
Distance:	5-mile loop.
Terrain:	Moderate climb to an area with lots of open descents.
Trail difficulty:	Novice to intermediate.
Surface quality:	Ungroomed, but often well tracked by skiers and snowshoers.
Elevation:	The trail starts at 10,549 feet; the highest elevation is at 11,000 feet.
Time:	3 to 4 hours.
Avalanche danger:	Low to moderate.
Snowmobile use:	Moderate.
Food and facilities:	Vail, 10 miles to the west of Vail Pass, is a great place to play and stay. Luxury hotels, bed-and-breakfasts, and condominiums are available. For information call the Vail/Beaver Creek Central Reservations (800–525–2257). Make sure you get your groceries, and drinks before leaving Vail. Food is not available once you get up onto Vail Pass.

I f you want to get a head start on the cross-country skiing or snowshoeing season, this is a great trail because it is in one of the areas that gets lots of snow early. Here you can enjoy the backcountry without actually being too far from the city. Corral Creek Trail is on the east side of I–70, and it's a sweet and relatively easy alternative to Shrine Pass Trail to the west, which gets so much snowmobile traffic. As with Shrine Pass and Commando Run, skiing in Corral Creek requires a day-use fee.

With a steep hill right at the start, this is a good trail if you are a novice skier or snowshoer who wants to hit it hard at first and then have a pleasant tour with gradual changes in elevation. From the parking lot cross over to the east side of I–70. The trail is not well marked so don't expect to see much more than other ski or snowshoe tracks heading northeast and climbing steadily up and around the hill. For the first 0.3 mile as you climb the hill, you'll gain about 200 vertical feet in elevation.

Crest or traverse the hill around to the northeast. Below you is the Corral Creek drainage area. There is plenty of open country in the drainage both to the north and south. Corral Creek Trail itself actually is the one that bends around to the south, following the creek. Here you can take advantage of the open and wide slopes of the drainage to prac-

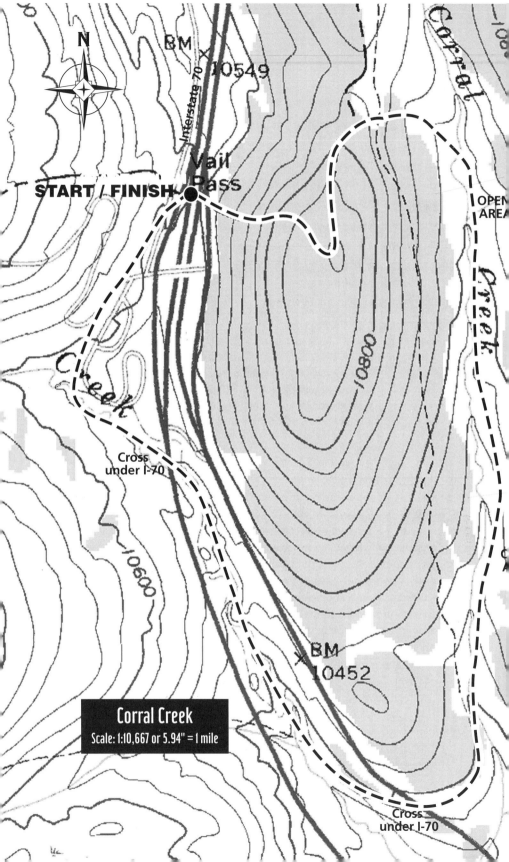

N

BM
× 10549

Interstate 70

Vail
Pass

START / FINISH

OPEN
AREA

Corral Creek

Creek

Cross
under I-70

10600

10800

BM
× 10452

Cross
under I-70

Corral Creek
Scale: 1:10,667 or 5.94" = 1 mile

tice carving turns or enjoy a downhill snowshoe jaunt. Feel free to ski off the trail, selecting any route you want. As long as you keep heading south, down the Corral Creek drainage area, you'll eventually loop around, and at the 2.75-mile point the trail hits its lowest point and actually crosses back under I–70.

The trail follows the divide literally between the north and south interstate. Catch the bike path heading north, paralleling the interstate and running in between the traffic above. Begin a gradual ascent for its last 1.5 miles. The trail ends right back at the parking lot on the west side of the interstate where you left your vehicle!

How to get there

From Denver go west on I–70 approximately 90 miles to exit 190 at Vail Pass. If you're coming from Vail, take I–70 east for about 10 miles to exit 190. Immediately after getting off the freeway, you'll see a large parking lot on the west side of the interstate. It's kept plowed all winter, and it has a rest stop and a warming hut.

Unlike most other areas found throughout Colorado that are open and free to the public for skiing and snowshoeing, Vail Pass is now part of a "fee demonstration area." You will have to pay a user fee. The money collected will be used to manage this heavy-use area. Self-fee tubes are available at all access points to the area. For information about the fees, call the Holy Cross Ranger district office at (970) 827–5715.

Directions at a glance

- The trail begins in the parking lot on the west side of I–70. (Pay your day-use fee!)
- Cross over to the east side of I–70.
- Climb the hill to the northeast.
- When you've reached the ridge, you'll see the large open Corral Creek drainage area.
- The trail goes downhill to the south.
- At 2.75 mile the trail crosses back under I–70.
- Take the bike path to the north, staying between northbound and southbound interstate traffic for approximately 1.5 miles.
- The trail turns into a road and will bring you back to the parking lot where you left your car.

Boreas Pass

White River National Forest, Breckenridge, CO

Type of trail:	▬▬ ⬭
Also used by:	Snowmobilers.
Distance:	7.2 miles to and from Baker's Tank; 13.4 miles to and from Boreas Pass and the Section House hut.
Terrain:	Moderate climbs along an old railroad bed all the way from the trailhead to the summit.
Trail difficulty:	Novice to intermediate.
Surface quality:	Ungroomed, but usually well tracked by skiers and snowshoers.
Elevation:	The trailhead is at 10,229 feet, and you will climb to 11,481 feet; elevation change 1,140 feet.
Time:	4 hours to all day.
Avalanche danger:	Low.
Snowmobile use:	Moderate.
Food and facilities:	There are no facilities along the trail. For day trips, bring food, snacks, and water from Breckenridge, where you'll find plenty of grocery stores, convenience stores, and fast-food restaurants. If you're planning to stay over at the Section House hut, bring food and sleeping bags with you. Advance reservations are a must and can be made by calling the 10th Mountain Division Hut Association at (970) 925–5775.

Boreas Pass was originally built as a wagon train road and was later used as the route for the nation's highest elevation, narrow-gauge railroad. From 1872 to 1938, a host of specially designed locomotives clanked along the tracks, handled the high altitudes, and ascended high grades and tight curves. In its time the railroad provided one of the most important means of transportation across the Continental Divide.

Today the remnants of the route provide winter enthusiasts with great cross-country skiing and snowshoeing opportunities. In this best of all worlds, you'll experience the joy of skiing and snowshoeing into and out of glade after glade of spruce, aspen, and fir trees. You'll also get an opportunity to traverse along a south-facing sunny route that follows the railroad grade and offers a gentle, continuous climb. This route is ideal if you are a beginning snowshoer or cross-country skier.

Two huts have been opened for snowshoers and skiers at the top of the pass. The Section House is named in honor of the railroad workers

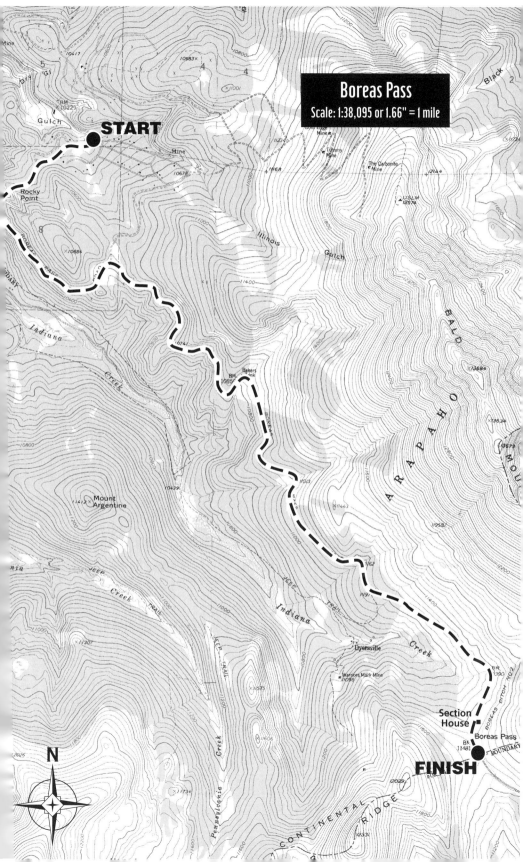

Boreas Pass
Scale: 1:38,095 or 1.66" = 1 mile

START

FINISH

N

The Section House at the top of Boreas Pass.

who took care of this section of track, and Ken's Cabin is named for Ken Graff, who was killed in an avalanche near Breckenridge in 1995. Ken's Cabin was built in the 1860s, the Section House in 1882, and both buildings were restored between 1992 and 1997 by the Summit Huts Association. The Section House is a 2,000-square-foot, two-story hewn log structure that can accommodate up to twelve skiers. Ken's Cabin is much smaller and sleeps two. Both cabins offer photovoltaic electricity, propane stoves, firewood, and all the usual hut amenities. Water is obtained by melting snow, so no dogs are allowed.

Reservations can be made for either hut through the 10th Mountain Division Hut Association. To stay overnight the Section House costs $26 per person, and Ken's Cabin goes for $69 for the whole hut. The use of the Section House and Ken's Cabin is for guests with advance reservations only. Please respect their privacy if you are climbing to Boreas Pass just for the day.

From the trailhead at the end of the plowed County Road 10, ski or snowshoe up Boreas Pass Road, the same route that was once used by Denver's South Park & Pacific Railroad. You'll immediately notice that you have spectacular views of the Blue River Valley and the majestic Tenmile Range. The route continues for nearly 0.5 mile, and then you'll reach Rocky Point, where more vistas of the Tenmile Range will greet you. You'll be able to look down and see the city of Breckenridge and the downhill ski runs to the west.

After almost 1.5 miles on the trail, the route continues its gradual climb in and out of tree stands and then makes a big S-turn, first to the left and then the right. Entering a clearing you'll see a trail that forks to the left. Continue on the main trail. Most of the route is gradual, but there are a couple of areas where the trail climbs more steeply. About 3.5 miles from the trailhead, the route will curve to the left and drop into a meadow, where there was once an old mining settlement. A few of the old structures should be visible through the snow.

Just ahead, and before you cross a small creek, you'll see historic Baker's Tank. In days gone by the old steam-powered locomotives would stop here and take on additional water for their boilers before continuing their trek up and over Boreas Pass. This is a natural place to stop for a break, enjoy the views, have lunch, and then turn around if you're not planning on continuing up to the pass.

If you are looking for a more strenuous workout and want to go all the way to the top of Boreas Pass, the route continues for another 3.6 miles past Baker's Tank to the summit of Boreas Pass. From here to the end, a large portion of this trail takes you above treeline. Although the trail is easy to follow, the lack of trees can make for plenty of windy hiking or skiing. Check the weather forecasts and try to choose a clear and calm day for this outing.

After you leave Baker's Tank, the trail continues much the same over the next mile. About 2 miles after Baker's Tank, you'll see a group of old buildings that made up the abandoned town of Dyersville. Unfortunately this is where you'll leave the shelter of

Directions at a glance

- From the trailhead at the end of the plowed Boreas Pass Road, continue up the old railroad grade.

- At 0.5 mile you've reached Rocky Point—great views of town down below.

- At 1.5 miles from the trailhead, the trail continues a gentle climb and twists left and right, ending up in a meadow. An old mining road forks to your left heading north.

- Stay on the main railroad bed to the 3.5-mile point; look out for old mining buildings.

- Go another 0.25 mile to Baker's Tank. Good lunch spot or turnaround point.

- If continuing to the summit or the Section House, continue to follow the main trail. Two miles past Baker's Tank are remnants of old buildings belonging to the abandoned town of Dyersville.

- After Dyersville you ski across open and gentle hillsides for the next 1.6 miles with very little tree cover. At the summit, look for the Section House and Ken's Cabin; they're easy to spot.

the big trees. As you continue your now easy-to-moderate climb, the last 1.5 miles or so brings you over open and gentle hillsides before the trail heads south. You'll climb steadily following the old railroad bed until it reaches the summit of Boreas Pass.

For the return trip you just go back the way you came, taking advantage of the gentle downhill, just about all the way back to your vehicle.

How to get there

From Denver go west on I–70 and take exit 203 to Frisco and Breckenridge. Go south on Colorado Highway 9 for approximately 10 miles and enter Breckenridge. At the southern end of town, turn left onto Boreas Pass Road (County Road 10). There will be a large sign explaining the history of Boreas Pass, located a short distance up the road. It makes interesting reading if you have the time to stop and digest it. If not, continue approximately 3.5 miles up County Road 10, as it winds up Illinois Gulch. The trail begins at the end of the road.

Peaks Trail

White River National Forest, Breckenridge, CO

Type of trail:	▬▬ 🔘
Distance:	10 miles one way; return shuttle service available.
Terrain:	Flat with gentle climbs and a fun descent at end of trail into Frisco.
Trail difficulty:	Intermediate.
Surface quality:	Ungroomed, but usually well tracked by skiers and snow-shoers.
Elevation:	The trailhead is in Breckenridge at 10,250 feet; the highest point is at 10,400 feet; and the trail ends at 9,561 feet in Frisco.
Time:	3 to 6 hours.
Avalanche danger:	Low.
Food and facilities:	Food and drinks can be found in Breckenridge and Frisco, depending on which way you plan to trek or ski the route. Both towns offer great dining for lunch and dinner, warm-up coffee or hot chocolate, and plenty of places for lounging, sightseeing, and shopping. If you plan to stay overnight in the area, call the Summit County Chamber of Commerce at (800) 530–3099. For shuttle information, routes, and times from Frisco to Breckenridge, call the Summit Stage at (970) 668–0999.

The Peaks Trail is a fun trail that links the two Colorado mountain towns of Breckenridge and Frisco over a 10-mile stretch that skirts the eastern slopes of the Tenmile Range. Although the trail can be done from both directions, the most popular route is to begin in Breckenridge and finish in Frisco. Even though the distance seems a little long for the advanced beginner or intermediate snowshoer or skier, the route is generally flat and has some nice downhill trekking or skiing sections.

It's also a very popular route for many winter users who don't want to partake in a full day of skiing or snowshoeing. Whenever they feel they've had enough of a workout, they can return to the trailhead at Breckenridge. If you want to trek or ski all the way from one town to the other, you can park a shuttle car. Or if you'd rather, there is free public transportation between Breckenridge and Frisco on the Summit Stage. Before you hit the trail, be sure to check with the Summit Stage folks about schedules and routes. Times and exact pickup and drop-off points vary throughout the season.

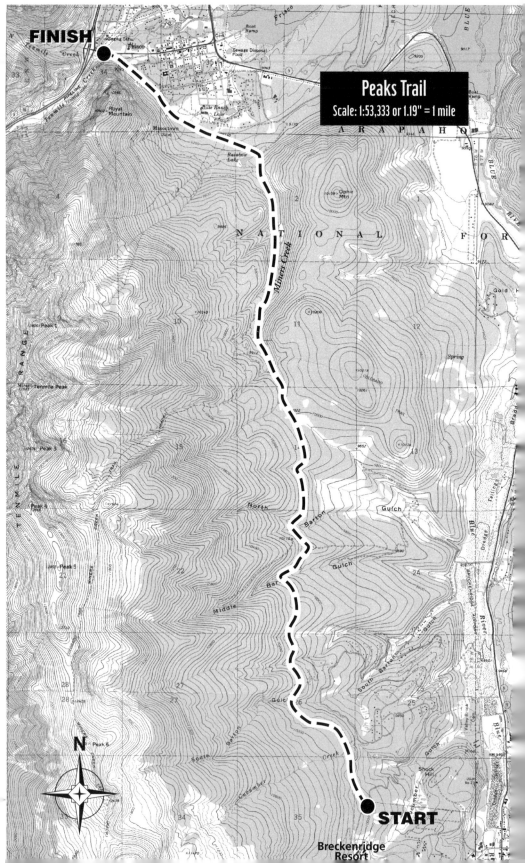

FINISH

Peaks Trail
Scale: 1:53,333 or 1.19" = 1 mile

N

START

Breckenridge
Resort

The easiest and most popular way to follow the Peaks Trail is to start in Breckenridge and head toward Frisco because the trail is very flat for the majority of the route and ends with a downhill into Frisco. After a long day of skiing, gliding, or snowshoe trekking, a good and final downhill run can be a welcome feature to a trail.

Well suited for cross-country skiers and showshoers, this trail is well marked with blue diamonds or red flagging tape and is a pleasure for beginners as well as skiers and snowshoers with more experience. The meadowlike clearings will provide you with some great opportunities to rest and take in the breathtaking views of Mount Baldy, Mount Gayot, and the Blue River Valley.

Regular users and visitors say that this is one of Colorado's best trails. First-timers love it because it's easy and not too crowded. Novices don't have to worry about competing for trail space with snowmobilers. On this 10-mile stretch snowmobiles are strictly prohibited, which makes the trail very peaceful and secluded. In addition because most of it is below treeline, it's sheltered from the wind and gives the user the true feeling of a gentle stroll through the woods.

From the Breckenridge trailhead the first part of the route weaves in and out of thick glades of trees. It's fairly wide and level with only a moderate climb before crossing Cucumber Creek. After the creek, about 0.5 mile from the trailhead, you will continue to ski or snowshoe north until descending into a clearing. The Forest Service harvested the trees and created this small meadow within the last few years to open it up for wildlife habitat and improve the health of the forest by creating age and size differences among the trees. The short-term benefit for you is that it has provided several open areas to play in.

Directions at a glance

- From the Breckenridge trailhead, the first 0.5 mile gently weaves through trees.
- Cross Cucumber Creek.
- Descend into a clearing cut by the Forest Service.
- At the junction in Middle Barton Gulch, take the left fork of the trail.
- Follow the trail north for several miles, passing North Barton Gulch and leaving tree cover for open meadows.
- For the last few miles, the trail heads northwest along the creek bed and then descends along Miners Creek.
- Stay on the trail and pass the sign to Rainbow Lake.
- At the T-intersection (0.25 mile past Rainbow Lake cutoff), turn left on the plowed road.
- Ski or hike about 0.5 mile until the road intersects Colorado Highway 9.
- Find the shuttle bus pickup point and enjoy a free ride back to Breckenridge.

Skiing through the trees.

Next you will come to a junction in the Middle Barton Gulch area. Take the left fork, staying on a well-established trail. Following the trail north for another couple of miles, you'll pass North Barton Gulch and leave the shelter of the trees, again skiing into some open meadows.

The last few miles of the trail descend along Miners Creek and then into the town of Frisco. During the winter and even spring, this last part of the route can get fast and icy. Of the entire journey, it's only the last couple of icy downhill miles that earns this route its intermediate rating.

While skiing into and along the Miners Creek Valley, stay on the road toward the north and meander in and out of the woods. Pass the sign to Rainbow Lake and stay on the main road. After you've passed the sign to Rainbow Lake, within 0.25 mile, you'll hit a T intersection where Miners Creek Road meets the Frisco-Breckenridge Bike Path. Make a left at the T-intersection and head west for about 2 miles until you reach Main Street near I–70 in Frisco. You may encounter snowmobiles on this section of the tour. As a result the trail surface will be groomed and possibly icy.

You can then walk to where you parked your shuttle vehicle at the west end of Frisco or simply look for the numerous signed shuttle bus stops along the route. A bus will pick you up and transport you back to the Breckenridge area.

How to get there

Take I–70 to exit 203 (Frisco and Breckenridge) and drive approximately 10 miles south on Colorado Highway 9. Once you are in downtown Breckenridge, you will come to the stop light in the middle of the town. Turn right onto Ski Hill Road (County Road 3). Continue on County Road 3 and drive past the Peak 8 base area of Breckenridge Resort for about another 0.5 mile. You'll come to a plowed area on the left side of the road that is marked with a PEAKS TRAIL sign.

On weekends and during the busy part of the ski season, you may have trouble finding a parking place. In this case, park at the bottom of Ski Hill Road in one of the Breckenridge off-site lots, and take the free shuttle to the base of Peak 8. From there you can walk to the trailhead.

To leave a shuttle car, take I–70 to exit 201 in Frisco. Turn left off the ramp and look for the public parking area on the right side of Main Street just past the overpass.

Francie's Cabin

White River National Forest, Breckenridge, CO

Type of trail:	═══ ⊛
Distance:	The easiest route to and from the cabin—6 miles; the more difficult route to and from the cabin—4.2 miles; the easiest route to and from the lake—8.2 miles; and the more difficult route to and from the lake—6.4 miles
Terrain:	Easy beginning and then steady and moderate climbs to the cabin and then the lake.
Trail difficulty:	Intermediate to advanced.
Surface quality:	Ungroomed but often well tracked by skiers and snowshoers.
Elevation:	Trailhead is at 10,180 feet; hut is at 11,300 feet.
Time:	3 to 5 hours.
Avalanche danger:	Low.
Food and facilities:	There are no facilities available on the trail. Load up with food, snacks, and water before leaving Breckenridge. The trail is only a couple miles south of town. If you're packing into Francie's Cabin for an overnight stay, make sure to bring groceries. The cabin has beds, firewood, lanterns, propane stove, and utensils. Make sure you bring your own sleeping bag. There is no day use at the cabin. Use of the hut, which includes decks, is by advance fee and reservation only. Day skiers should respect the privacy of Francie's Cabin guests by keeping their distance from the hut. Call the 10th Mountain Division Hut Association at (970) 925-5775.

Francie's Cabin is one of three huts built by the Summit Huts Association. It has quickly become a popular destination because of its proximity to Spruce and Crystal Creeks, wonderful backcountry areas for ski touring and snowshoeing. There are two ways to get there: Either use Spruce Creek Road or Crystal Creek Trail. If you want a relatively easy trip from the trailhead, take Spruce Creek Road. It's a gentle road that was built for summer travel; it's easy to follow, fast, and takes you right to the cabin.

If you feel a little wild and want the challenge of a good stiff climb on the inbound route or steep descents on the outbound leg of the trip, take Crystal Creek Trail. With an elevation change of over 750 feet in just 1 mile, this old four-wheel-drive road gives the skier plenty of thrills . . . or spills. Climbing skins are a must, and the route may be well suited for snowshoers who don't have to worry about slipping backward.

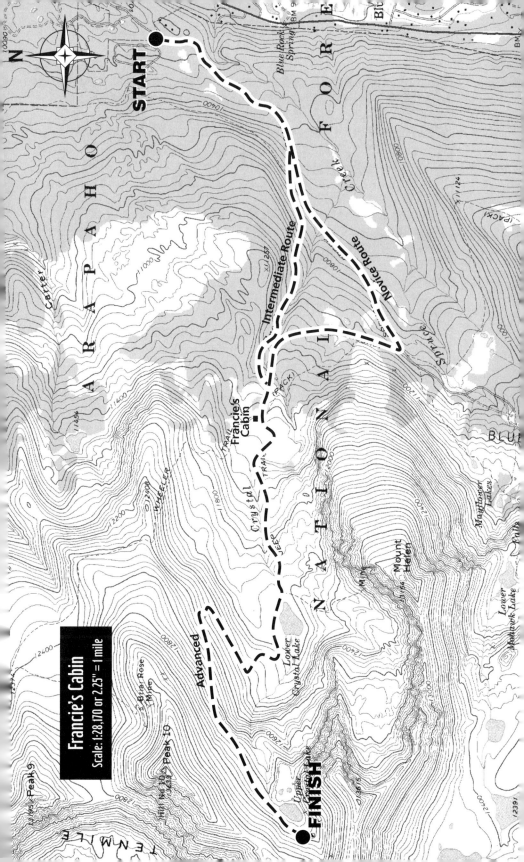

Francie's Cabin.

To access both routes, begin skiing or snowshoeing southwest along Spruce Creek Road. Snowmobiles are allowed along Spruce Creek Road, but they are not allowed around the hut. The road climbs gradually and will intersect Crystal Creek Trail about 1 mile from the trailhead. If you decide to take on the challenge of a hard climb, head west on Crystal Creek Trail. You'll go approximately 1.3 miles and intersect with Wheeler Trail right before you reach Francie's Cabin.

If you decide on the more gentle route, stay on Spruce Creek Road for another 1 mile, heading southwest. At that point, you'll see an aqueduct road running north and south. Turn right, heading north. The aqueduct will gradually bend around to the northwest and meet up with Wheeler Trail. Blue diamond blazes will show you the way to the cabin.

If you don't have reservations to stay at the cabin and want to further explore the area, keep going west up Crystal Creek Valley for about 1 mile, and you'll come to Lower Crystal Lake. There you'll find the remnants of a silver mining operation that dates back to the late 1800s and early 1900s. A magnificent view of Mount Helen, which stretches 13,164 feet into the sky, can be seen to the south. This area was also once heavily mined and yielded a lot of lead-based ores. It now yields spectacular views of craggy peaks.

If you want to press on, you can continue to ski or snowshoe on the four-wheel-drive Crystal Creek Trail. To reach the end of the trail, it's just under 2 miles, but it is a steep climb and is recommended for advanced skiers and snowshoers in very good physical condition. Past Lower Crystal Lake follow the gradual slope to the right, then the road traverses to the

Directions at a glance

- From the trailhead go southwest 1 mile on Spruce Creek Road.
- At the 1-mile point, look for the cutoff to the right heading west. This is Crystal Creek Trail.
- For the easiest route stay on Spruce Creek Road another 1 mile, heading southwest.
- Two miles from the trailhead, you'll see an aqueduct road. Turn right and head north.
- Take the aqueduct road north for approximately 0.75 mile. Where it meets Wheeler Trail, look for blue diamonds that will lead you to Francie's Cabin.

Alternate route

- From the trailhead go southwest 1 mile on Spruce Creek Road.
- At approximately 1 mile, look for Crystal Creek Trail, which cuts off on your right to the west.
- If you take this more advanced trail, plan on some steeper climbing.
- When it crosses Wheeler Trail, look for blue diamonds that will lead you to the cabin.

right across a steeper slope. After about 0.25 mile the road turns back across the slope to reach the bench where Upper Crystal Lake sits at 12,850 feet.

If you are making a day trip and want to stop and rest around Francie's Cabin, please respect the privacy of the guests staying there. The use of the cabin, including the decks, is by reservation only. Dogs are not allowed because the water for the cabin is obtained by melting snow that's retrieved from outside. Overnight stays are $28 (plus tax) per person and include all the basic amenities—beds, firewood, cooking supplies, etc.

When you return retrace the route down Spring Creek Road for the mild tour, or go down the Crystal Creek Trail for a wild descent!

How to get there

Take I–70 west from Denver to exit 203 (Frisco and Breckenridge). From the exit go south on Colorado Highway 9 approximately 10 miles to downtown Breckenridge. From downtown Breckenridge drive south on Colorado Highway 9 for approximately 2 miles to Spruce Creek Road (County Road 800). Signs will direct you to make a right turn at the turnoff. Head west on Spruce Creek Road for about 0.5 to 0.75 mile, until you reach the end of the plowed road. Use the Spruce Creek trailhead area for parking.

Janet's Cabin

White River National Forest, Copper Mountain, CO

Type of trail: ▬▬ ◉

Also used by: First portion—0.25 mile—used by downhill skiers at Copper Mountain Resort.

Distance: 9.2 miles to and from Union Creek trailhead; or 7.6 miles when taking ski lift to the mountaintop.

Terrain: Steady and gentle climbs to the cabin and an easy glide or trek downhill back to the trailhead.

Trail difficulty: Novice to intermediate.

Surface quality: Ungroomed, but usually well tracked by skiers or snowshoers.

Elevation: Union Creek trailhead is at 9,820 feet; Janet's Cabin is at 11,610 feet

Time: 3 to 5 hours.

Avalanche danger: Low.

Food and facilities: Cross-country and snowshoe rentals, lodging, restaurants, a convenience store, rest rooms, and repair shop are all available at the Union Creek area of Copper Mountain Resort (970–968–2882). Be sure to check with Copper about the grooming status of trails and whether K and L lifts are running. Use of Janet's Cabin, including the decks and picnic tables, is by advance reservation and fee only. Day skiers should respect the privacy of Janet's Cabin guests by keeping their distance from the hut. Obtain additional information or reservations for use of Janet's Cabin by calling the 10th Mountain Division Hut Association at (303) 925–5775. Groceries for an extended stay are best picked up in Frisco, 8 miles east off I–70.

Janet's Cabin is one of the area's most popular huts, partly because its trailhead is conveniently located close to the Denver metro area at Copper Mountain Resort.

Nestled in the trees near the head of Guller Creek along the Colorado Trail, Janet's Cabin was built in 1990 and is a memorial to Janet Boyd Tyler, a Vail resident who was active in Colorado skiing for many years before she died of cancer in 1988. This area was also a favorite training ground for the 10th Mountain Division, elite ski troops during World War II.

The trail invites skiers of all abilities because it is short and easy to follow. It's ideal for day skiers who want the experience of backcountry

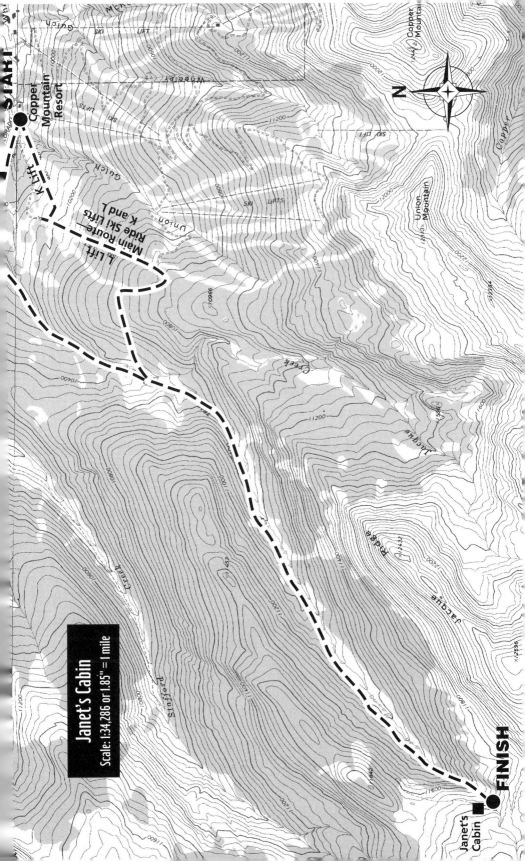

Just before the last big pull to Janet's Cabin.

skiing without having to stay overnight in the hut. Day trips along this trail are often what skiers and snowshoers opt for, so the trail can sometimes be crowded.

For telemark skiers, snowboarders, or industrious snowshoers, there are incredible bowls above the cabin near Searle Pass and Sugarloaf Mountain ideal for carving turns or exploring. Like many trails in the area, the region is popular with snowboarders looking for open, uncrowded, and unused deep powder areas. Many snowshoers trekking into the area are often armed with a backpack that includes not only day supplies but a snowboard as well!

The cabin itself is a 2,700-square-foot log structure that offers a propane stove and burners, photovoltaic system for lighting, indoor odorless toilets, a detached sauna, and cooking facilities, including utensils. The

---

Directions at a glance

- If you are staying at Janet's Cabin, take the K or L chair lift to the top of the Union Creek area of Copper Mountain Resort.

- Ski less than 0.25 mile down the West Tenmile ski slope, then look for the national forest access gate on the left.

- Ski downhill on Elk Track Trail to the junction of the Colorado Trail at Guller Creek.

- Ski southwest on the Colorado Trail following Guller Creek for just over 2.6 miles.

- Climb a steep hill (400 vertical feet) to the cabin in last 0.25 mile.

- To return, follow the same route back down Guller Creek. Climb the hill back to the access gate on the West Tenmile ski slope. Ski down the slope to the parking lot at Union Creek.

Alternate route (for day skiers or snowshoers)

- Go west on the trail from the Union Creek base area at Copper Mountain Resort. Be sure to call ahead to confirm the grooming status of the cross-country trails.

- Intersect the Colorado Trail at Guller Creek and go left.

- Ski the Colorado Trail along Guller Creek for approximately 3.7 miles.

- Climb a steep hill (400 vertical feet) to the cabin in the last 0.25 mile.

- To return—follow the same route back down Guller Creek. Climb the hill to the right that will take you to an access gate on the West Tenmile ski slope. Ski down the slope to the Union Creek parking lot.

Janet's Cabin.

large facilities are rustic but very nicely appointed. Janet's Cabin has four bedrooms and can sleep up to twenty overnight guests.

Over the last few years Copper Mountain Resort has expanded its base lodges and facilities extensively. As a result, all the parking lots close to the mountain now require a fee. This includes Union Creek, the closest parking lot to the trailhead for Janet's Cabin. For free parking use the East Lot near Colorado Highway 91 and take the free shuttle to Union Creek.

If you are an overnight guest with reservations, you'll be issued a ride pass that's good for a one-way trip up the K and L chair lifts. From the base of the chair lift, simply board for two short rides to the top of the Union Creek area. From there follow the signs down the west edge of the "beginner" trail, West Tenmile. You'll soon see the public access gate to the White River National Forest. At the forest access, you'll ski down Elk Track Trail, a mostly gentle route with only a few steep descents through the trees. Soon you'll meet the Colorado Trail/Guller Creek Trail and follow that for about 2 miles, skiing through meadows and forests, moderately gaining elevation. Just before the 3-mile point, you'll cross over a meadow and travel another 0.6 mile southwest. Here the trail to Janet's Cabin, marked with blue diamonds, leaves the Colorado Trail. It is only used during the winter. At about 0.25 mile from Janet's Cabin, you'll encounter a steep hill where you'll climb 400 feet in elevation to reach the hut. It's the last 0.5 mile, where the terrain becomes steep climbing, that gives this route its advanced beginner to intermediate rating.

If you're day skiing or snowshoeing only, free ski lift passes are obviously not provided, and you'll have to take the longer 5-mile route. From the Cross-Country Center at Copper Mountain, the trail starts on the side of the building. Hike or ski to the west end of the ski area and look for the public access sign. You'll be skiing or trekking across a downhill ski run, so watch for fast moving downhill skiers. Continue west until you intersect the Colorado Trail and then turn left. The trail follows along Guller Creek in a southwest direction. It's about 3.7 miles up the Colorado Trail and the climb is steady.

Please note that all of the Janet's Cabin facilities are *not* for use by day skiers, snowshoers, or snowboarders. Only skiers who are guests with reservations are allowed to use the cabin's rest rooms and other facilities, others and are asked to stay away from the cabin and respect the privacy of guests.

How to get there

From Denver, take I–70 west to exit 195 (Colorado Highway 91) and go south less than 0.25 mile to the main entrance of Copper Mountain Resort. Turn west onto the resort road. Take the first left into the East Lot and drive to the end of the parking area. If you've made reservations for an overnight stay at Janet's Cabin, look for the designated overnight parking slots. Otherwise do not park in these spots—they are for guests with reservations only. Take the free resort shuttle to Union Creek. Overnight guests should then proceed to the Union Creek ticket window for lift passes. Remember to bring your hut reservation as proof you are staying overnight.

Wheeler Lakes

White River National Forest, Copper Mountain, CO

Type of trail:	▬▬ ⬭
Distance:	4 miles.
Terrain:	Steep and challenging climbs from the trailhead to Wheeler Lakes, with steep descents back to the trailhead.
Trail difficulty:	Advanced.
Surface quality:	Ungroomed backcountry conditions, and usually not well tracked by skiers or snowshoers.
Elevation:	The trail starts at about 9,720 feet, climbs to 11,050 feet; elevation changes more than 1,200 feet.
Time:	3 to 5 hours.
Avalanche danger:	Low.
Food and facilities:	There is no food, water, or even rest rooms. Gas and a convenience store can be found just south of I–70 on Colorado Highway 91 for snacks, water, and soft drinks. Restaurants and lodging can also be found just south of I–70 on Colorado Highway 91 at Copper Mountain Resort (800–958–8386) or east on I–70 in Frisco or Silverthorne. Call the Summit County Chamber of Commerce at (800) 530–3099. You'll find fast food, grocery stores, fancy dining, and plenty of accommodations in either of these towns.

Wheeler Lakes Trail, which leads summer and winter users up to the high alpine lakes, is difficult both physically and because it requires navigating through deep snows with minimal trail markings. It's a trail that should only be attempted by advanced skiers or snowshoers. If you are out of shape, not an expert skier or snowshoer, and don't possess excellent backcountry skills, you may want to try an easier trail first!

Wheeler Lakes Trail is also part of the Dillon-Wheeler Trail, which connects to the Gore Range Trail. The Gore Range Trail rolls up and over the eastern slopes of the Gore Range for more than 50 miles all the way to Heeney near Green Mountain Reservoir. The avalanche danger is rated as low, but the trail does climb just over 1,300 feet in less than 2 miles from the trailhead and quickly leaves civilization behind. In less than 0.5 mile, you enter the Eagle's Nest Wilderness Area, where no mechanized or motorized vehicle traffic is allowed. Often during the winter, deep snow completely covers markers, making the trail difficult to follow and sometimes impossible to find! Solid map-reading and compass skills are a must.

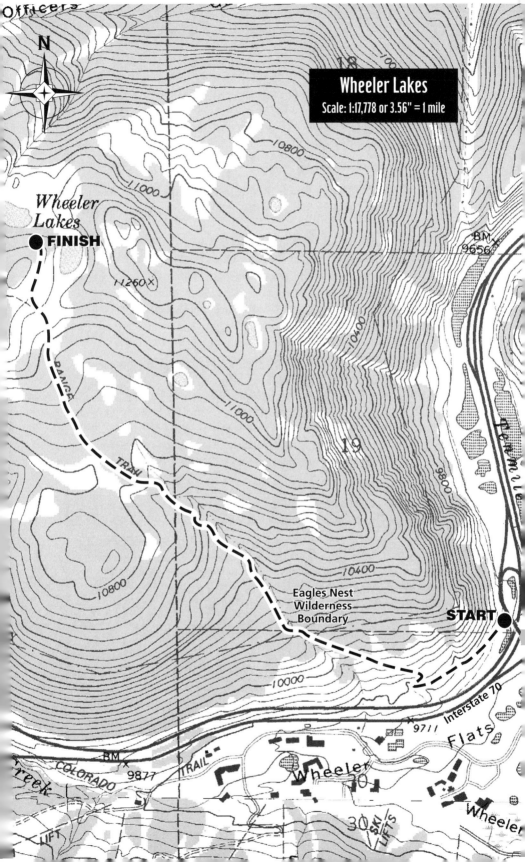

During the summer months when the snows have melted, the Gore Range Trail to Wheeler Lakes is a popular route for backpackers and hikers heading for the lakes. During the winter months you don't have to follow the summer trail. As we said previously, chances are excellent that it's going to be hidden and often hard to find. However, if you want to challenge yourself, the rewards of deep powder and meadows all along the steep hills and the trail are phenomenal. Inside the Eagle's Nest Wilderness Area, the remoteness and quiet are in stark contrast to the bustling sounds of close-by Copper Mountain Resort and the heavy traffic on I–70.

From the trailhead near the Colorado Highway 91 exit from I–70, go southwest approximately 0.2 mile through thick stands of aspen trees. Look for a trailhead sign at this point and head southwest, following the contour of the hill around to the south-facing slope above I–70. Approximately 0.5 mile around the bend, look for a small gully that heads uphill and to the left. There is a wooden Forest Service sign posted high enough on a tree by the trail that it doesn't get buried by deep snows. It marks the beginning of the Eagles Nest Wilderness Area.

From here the trail follows the gulley to the northwest. By the 1-mile point, you'll climb to 10,000 feet and see magnificent views of the Tenmile Range to the east and Jacques Peak and Machine Gun Ridge to the west. Below you to the south is the ski resort. As you continue north-

Directions at a glance

- From the trailhead near Colorado Highway 91, go southwest approximately 0.2 mile through thick stands of aspen trees.
- Look for trailhead sign at this point and head northwest. Approximately 0.5 mile up the trail, look for a Forest Service sign along trail, high above deep snow level. You've now reached the Eagle's Nest Wilderness Area.
- The trail turns northwest and continues its steep climb.
- When the aspen forest turns to conifer, you've reached the halfway point.
- The trail veers more sharply north for next 0.5 mile and continues for just over another 0.5 mile.
- Look for the intersection to Wheeler Lakes. The Forest Service has posted a wooden sign here, and Wheeler Lakes is about 0.25 mile to the northeast.
- Take your time returning on the trail exactly as you came up.

northwest on the trail, you will climb steadily and begin to hike or ski in and out of dense glades of conifers. When the aspens give way to the evergreens, you know that you are near the halfway point to the lakes.

The trail begins to flatten out. Soon afterward it will head to the north over hilly meadows for another 0.5 mile. Keep a lookout for the intersection at the Dillon-Wheeler Trail and Wheeler Lakes. Again it's marked by a wooden Forest Service sign that should be nailed to a tree above the deep snow levels. If you don't find it, don't fret. The Wheeler Lakes are just ahead a little to the northeast, and you made it. For a great view of the Gore Range and the northern end of the Tenmile Range, continue past the lakes to the point where the slope drops away toward Officers Gulch.

Return on the trail the same way you came up. Downhill snowshoe trekking or skiing may be pretty thrilling since some spots are going to be steep. Take your time going up, and doubly take your time coming back down!

How to get there

Take I–70 west from Denver to Vail and then take exit 195 onto Colorado Highway 91. Immediately after exiting I–70, you'll see the overpass off the designated off-ramp. Slow down and look for a parking area on the right before the overpass over I–70.

Look for a small dirt turnout area, and if there's room, park here. Unfortunately it only accommodates a couple of cars or one big truck. If there's no room to park, drive across the overpass, park in the East Lot at Copper Mountain Resort, and walk back to the trailhead. Be careful of vehicles traveling fast coming off I–70.

Tennessee Pass Cookhouse (Dinner Yurt)

San Isabel National Forest, Ski Cooper, CO

Type of trail:	═══ ⬤ ⊰
Also used by:	Snowmobilers.
Distance:	2 miles.
Terrain:	Easy climb up to the cookhouse and gentle glide back down to the ski resort.
Trail difficulty:	Novice.
Surface quality:	Groomed and always tracked by skiers and snowshoers.
Elevation:	The trail starts at 10,537 feet and climbs to 10,797 at the cookhouse.
Time:	30 minutes.
Food and facilities:	Because it's such a short "fun-run" to the cookhouse, few if any advance preparations are going to be required. If you're going to stay in Vail and come 30 miles south for the dinner trek, it's advised that you make advance reservations for accommodations in the Vail area. You can get brochure information on all overnight facilities by calling the Vail/Beaver Creek Reservations at (800) 525–2257. Vail also has a host of grocery stores, convenience stores, gas stations, and superb restaurants.

A more moderately priced option to Vail is a stay in Leadville, located less than 10 miles south from the Tennessee Pass trailhead. Hotel, motel, and bed-and-breakfast information is available by calling the Leadville Chamber of Commerce at (719) 486–3900. Leadville also has grocery stores, gas stations, and restaurants.

The Tennessee Pass Cookhouse can accommodate about thirty guests per evening. The package price of $55 per person also includes all your cross-country ski or snowshoe equipment, guides, headlamps, and dinner. Taxes, gratuities, and your bar tab are extra. For further information or reservations (which are a must!), call (719) 486–1750.

This is not our usual backcountry trail since Bill's Trail starts at Piney Creek Nordic Center and has really only one purpose—to take skiers and snowshoers to the Tennessee Pass Cookhouse. What makes this destination so unique is that it is the only gourmet restaurant in Colorado that's a yurt tucked back in the forest! Adhering to Forest Service policy that structures in this area must be temporary, the people at the nordic

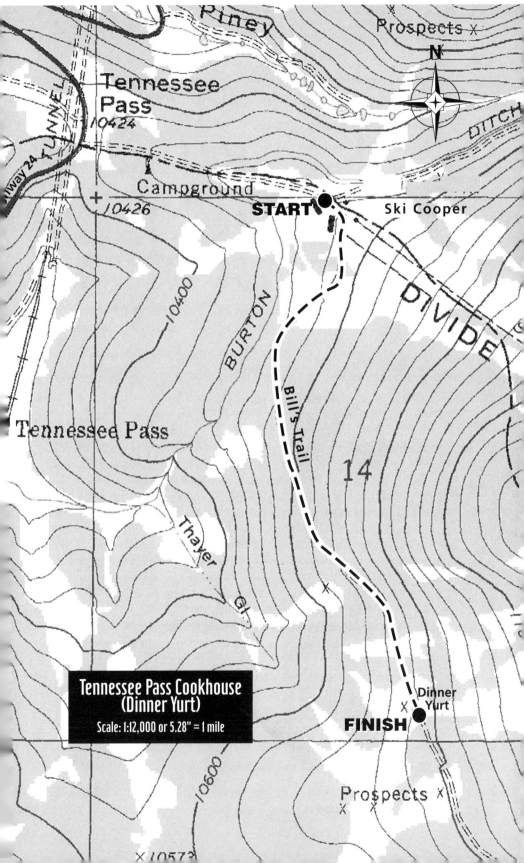

Piney

Prospects ×

N

Tennessee
Pass
10424

ΤUNNEL

Iway 24

DITCH

Campground

START

Ski Cooper

10426

DIVIDE

BURTON

10400

Bill's Trail

Tennessee Pass

14

Thayer Gl.

Dinner
Yurt

Tennessee Pass Cookhouse
(Dinner Yurt)

Scale: 1:12,000 or 5.28" = 1 mile

FINISH

10600

× 10573

Prospects ×

× ×

center decided a yurt built on eaves would do the trick. It's literally a gourmet restaurant that is temporarily permanent. Beginning around Thanksgiving each year, the cookhouse opens for evening dinner guests and stays open until about the middle of April.

After a hard day of skiing or snowshoeing at the numerous backcountry areas in and around the Tennessee Pass area, a day of alpine skiing at Ski Cooper, or just visiting the scenic sights around Leadville—how about sitting down to a sumptuous four-course dinner following a quick 15- to 30-minute cross-country ski or snowshoe trip? It's a trip that is both unusual and highly satisfying.

Bill's Trail to the Tennessee Pass Cookhouse is a standard 10-foot-wide path and meanders south and east across gentle rolling hills strewn with heavy woods along Cooper Loop Trail. It's ideal for beginners because it gains only about 300 feet in elevation in just over 1.25 miles.

After leaving Piney Creek Nordic Center at Ski Cooper, you head south along a well-marked trail. Continue south and then go east for about 0.75 mile. After you break out from the trees at the top of the hill, you'll see the yurt in an open meadow. Park your skis and walk to the deck where spectacular views of Mounts Elbert and Massive, the highest and second highest peaks in Colorado, greet you. Not to be outdone by the big tops, Homestake Peak and Galena Peak also fill your view, as well as Mounts Sherman, Evans, and Sheridan of the Mosquito Range.

The trail, part of the larger Cooper Loop Trail, which is in turn part of the Forest Service system, is regularly groomed and ideal for skating or classic touring. Snowmobiles are also available to take disabled skiers or snowshoers and other visitors along the trail.

Guides will lead the group to the Tennessee Pass Cookhouse each afternoon at 5:30 P.M. for the cookhouse's single seating. Be sure to make your reservations and choose your entree ahead of time. Organized guided tours return about 9:00 P.M. However, if you want to finish dinner and return early or hit the trails for a little private skiing or snowshoeing, you're welcome to use your headlamp and enjoy the star-filled night sky.

Directions at a glance

- The trailhead begins at the Piney Creek Nordic Center.

- Head south and then east along Bill's Trail approximately 1 mile to the Tennessee Pass Cookhouse.

- Enjoy a gourmet dinner and return to the trailhead back along the same route.

Snowshoeing near Tennessee Pass.

How to get there

From Denver go west on I–70 approximately 105 miles to exit 171 and Minturn. This exit is approximately 5.4 miles west of Vail. At the bottom of the off-ramp, make a right and head south on U.S. Highway 24. Go approximately 24.5 miles to the top of Tennessee Pass. The turnoff to Ski Cooper is on your left at the top of the pass. Park by Piney Creek Nordic Center.

From Leadville go north on U.S. Highway 24 approximately 8.8 miles to Ski Cooper and turn right. Drive to Piney Creek Nordic Center and park. Check in at the nordic center.

Treeline Loop

San Isabel National Forest, Tennessee Pass, CO

Type of trail:	▬▬▬ 🟤
Also used by:	Snowmobilers.
Distance:	2.3 miles.
Terrain:	Easy climbs and descents while meandering through lots of tree groves.
Trail difficulty:	Novice.
Surface quality:	Ungroomed, but often tracked by skiers and snowshoers.
Elevation:	The trailhead is at 10,424 feet, and you will climb to over 10,640 feet at the 1-mile point.
Time:	2 to 3 hours.
Avalanche danger:	Low.
Snowmobile use:	Low.
Food and facilities:	It's less than 30 miles from Vail to the trailhead, and with some advance planning and reservations, there are usually accommodations—however pricey—available. You can get brochure information on all of the overnight facilities by calling the Vail/Beaver Creek Reservations at (800) 525–2257. Vail also has a host of grocery stores, convenience stores, gas stations, and superb restaurants to select from.

A more moderately priced option is to stay in Leadville, located less than 9 miles from the Treeline Loop trailhead. Hotel, motel, and bed-and-breakfast brochure information is available by calling the Leadville Chamber of Commerce at (719) 486–3900.

Complete equipment rentals and repairs can be found literally across the road at Piney Creek Nordic Center located at Ski Cooper. For information on tours, guides, and equipment, call (719) 486–1750.

If you're coming in from the north, make sure you secure your gas, groceries, water, and snacks before leaving the Vail area. Likewise if you're coming from Leadville. Once you head off on Treeline Loop Trail, there are no facilities.

The backcountry ski and snowshoe trails west of Tennessee Pass are notoriously underutilized. Unlike the Front Range trails, which are near heavily populated areas, the trails around Leadville see relatively few people and afford skiers and snowshoers the full experience of the uncrowded great outdoors. Breaking trail is often necessary and part

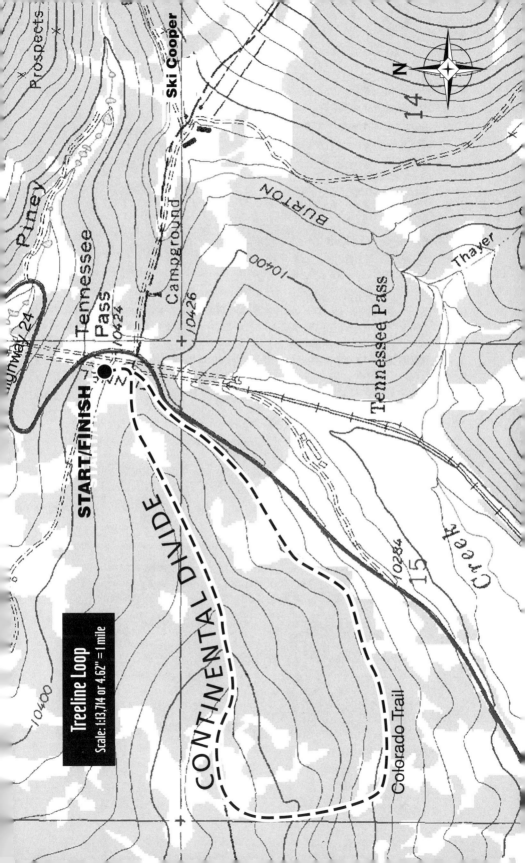

Prospects

Ski Cooper

N

14

Piney

Tennessee Pass

BURTON

Campground

10400

10426

10424

Tennessee Pass

Thayer

Highway 24

START/FINISH

CONTINENTAL DIVIDE

10284

15

Creek

Colorado Trail

Treeline Loop
Scale: 1:13,714 or 4.62" = 1 mile

10400

10400

of the joy of being the only group on the trail. Along with the solitude comes the need to possess good winter backcountry travel skills, as well as solid map-reading and compass knowledge.

As its name implies, Treeline Loop Trail meanders mainly within glades of trees. Shaded from the wind, it is a fun, not-too-demanding trail with gentle ascents and descents that let you experience the remoteness of the backcountry without having to be too far from civilization.

There are no spectacular views of mountains here. The allure of Treeline Loop Trail rests in being able to experience the uncrowded forest and the quiet of nature. If you are observant in early morning or late afternoon, you might see a snowshoe hare, a por-

Directions at a glance

- Follow the old Railroad Bed Road from the trailhead. Signs will indicate it's the start of Treeline Loop Trail.

- Go 0.25 mile south on the old Railroad Bed Road and then turn west onto Treeline Loop Trail.

- The trail literally follows along the top of the Continental Divide for approximately 1 mile.

- At the 1-mile mark, look for signs and a trail that turns left and heads south.

- Go 0.25 mile south heading downhill until you intersect the Colorado Trail.

- Make a left and head east 1 mile on the Colorado Trail as it loops back to the trailhead.

A view of Ski Cooper.

A Tennessee Pass meadow.

cupine, or squirrels, and you might hear the call of birds that live in the area. Certainly telltale tracks in the snow will attest to deer, elk, and other wildlife also living nearby.

From the Tennessee Pass trailhead, Treeline Loop Trail follows the old Railroad Bed Road south for a short distance and then intersects with the Continental Divide. Follow the signs along the Railroad Bed Road for a short distance, watching for the signs that will direct you west along the Divide. Quite literally for the 1 mile you're traveling west, you can plant one ski or snowshoe on the eastern side of the Rocky Mountains and the other on the western side. Talk about being able to enjoy a case of Rocky Mountain split personality!

After heading west for about 1 mile, look for a sign that will direct you to take the trail to the left heading south. Crossing just about anywhere in this general area will lead you gently downhill, and you'll intersect the Colorado Trail in less than 0.25 mile. On the way there you'll climb over a couple of small hills and cross a meadow.

When you intersect the Colorado Trail, make another left and head east. Again, it's a gentle traverse across the hillside for about 1 mile, and you will loop back around to the Tennessee Pass area. Once you're back at the trailhead, it's simple to cross the road and ski or snowshoe another 0.3 mile over to Ski Cooper for a warming cup of coffee or hot chocolate.

How to get there

From Denver go west on I–70 for approximately 105 miles to exit 171 and Minturn. This exit is approximately 5.4 miles west of Vail. At the bottom of the off-ramp, turn right and head south on U.S. Highway 24. Go approximately 24.5 miles to the top of Tennessee Pass. Park on the west side of U.S. Highway 24. If there's no parking available, make a left into Ski Cooper and park there.

From Leadville take U.S. Highway 24 north for 8.8 miles to Tennessee Pass. The trailhead is located on the west side of U.S. Highway 24 along the Continental Divide. Or if you want to add an additional 0.3 mile to your route, you can park at Ski Cooper and start the trail from Piney Creek Nordic Center.

10th Mountain Division Hut

San Isabel National Forest, Leadville, CO

Type of trail: ▬▬▬ ⬬

Also used by: Snowboarders.

Distance: 9 miles.

Terrain: Challenging climbs and descents to the hut, with great open bowls for skiing or trekking.

Trail difficulty: Intermediate.

Surface quality: Ungroomed, but sometimes tracked by skiers and snowshoers.

Elevation: Crane Park trailhead is at 10,137 feet and the hut is at 11,370 feet.

Time: 5 to 7 hours.

Snowmobile use: Low in area.

Food and facilities: It's recommended that the route to the 10th Mountain Division Hut be a destination point rather than a day trip. To make it to the hut, you may want to stay over in either Vail or Leadville the night before beginning your trek to the hut. For reservations and information about the other huts in the system, call (970) 925–5775. Advance reservations to stay over or use any of the facilities are required. The huts are open for reservations from Thanksgiving until the end of April, and the cost is $26 per person (plus tax), per night.

It's less than 30 miles from Vail to the trailhead, and with some advance planning and reservations, there are usually accommodations available. You can get brochure information on all of the overnight facilities by calling the Vail/Beaver Creek Reservations at (800) 525–2257. Vail also has a host of grocery stores, convenience stores, gas stations, and superb restaurants to select from.

A more moderately priced option is to stay in Leadville. Located less than 8 miles from the Crane Park trailhead, the accommodations and restaurant choices are not as "glitzy" as those found in Vail but are certainly a lot more affordable. Hotel, motel, and bed-and-breakfast brochure information is available by calling the Leadville Chamber of Commerce at (719) 486–3900.

If you're coming from the north, make sure you secure your gas, groceries, water, and snacks before leaving the Vail area. If you're coming from Leadville, you'll also find the same facilities. Once you head off on the trail from Crane Park, there are no facilities.

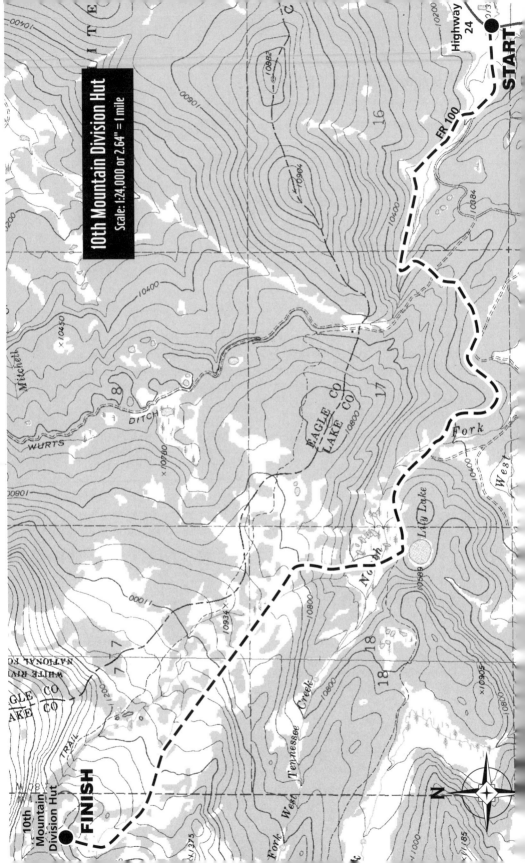

This area is the home of the illustrious 10th Mountain Division Hut System. The area surrounding the town of Leadville is historically important in the genesis of the sport of backcountry skiing in America. In 1942 the U.S. Army established Camp Hale just north of Leadville to house the 10th Mountain Division, an elite ski corps of commandos who trained for mountain combat against the Nazis in the European Alps. Also stationed there was the 99th Infantry Division. Made up of Norwegians and Norwegian expatriates, it was the only American division that included foreign citizens and was formed to aid the planned invasion of Norway.

For three winters, from 1942 to 1945, over 15,000 troops were stationed at Camp Hale. Unlike today's lightweight skis and gear, these commandos had to wear 7-foot skis and 90-pound packs. Camouflaged in winter-white suits, these "phantoms of the snow" practiced military exercises around what is now Ski Cooper and along the Gore and Sawatch Ranges under conditions of military secrecy that would rival today's top secret training bases!

After the war, many of these soldiers came back to the Rocky Mountains where they had trained. Continuing to ski, they became instrumental in popularizing cross-country skiing as a sport and were often the major forces behind the development of many of the Colorado ski resorts. In 1982 the first 10th Mountain Division Hut was erected. Today there are twelve huts, and the system is renowned as the most extensive and well laid-out of any in Colorado.

The overall favorite among strong backcountry skiers and snowshoers in the Leadville area is the trail to the 10th Mountain Division Hut—a hut and trail

Directions at a glance

- The trailhead begins at the Crane Park turnout area and is marked as Forest Road 100.

- Ski or trek west on Forest Road 100 for approximately 1 mile and look for Wurt's Ditch Road to intersect Forest Road 100 from the north.

- Continue on Forest Road 100 south and west for another 0.5 mile to the road that heads northwest to Lily Lake.

- A gentle ascent will take you over the North Fork of West Tennessee Creek and around the north side of Lily Lake.

- On north side of Lily Lake, look for a meadow on your right side (north).

- Ski across the meadow and pick up the trail to Slide Creek and Slide Lake.

- Watch for blue diamonds on the trees.

- Follow the blue diamonds to the 10th Mountain Division Hut.

- Return on the same trail used to come into the area.

Look for blue diamonds on the way to the 10th Mountain Division Hut.

that offer magnificent vistas of the 13,209-foot Homestake Peak to the west. Surrounding the hut are also great areas with deep powder ideal for practicing telemark turns, snowshoe treks, and even some open bowl snowboarding. As with all the huts, the usual course of action is to spend the night there. The 10th Mountain Division Hut offers accommodations for up to sixteen overnight skiers or snowshoers along with the standard cookstove, ice shovels, firewood, etc.

From the west side of U.S. Highway 24 at the Crane Park turnout, look for the Forest Service sign to Slide Lake Trail. It will be marked as Forest Road 100. Ski or snowshoe west on Forest Road 100 about 1 mile. Forest Road 100 road will intersect with Wurt's Ditch Trail from the right. This trail comes from the top of Tennessee Pass. Turn left on the road, which will follow the contour of the hill to a broad wooded ridge and another trail junction.

At approximately the 1.5-mile mark from the trailhead, take the road to the right heading northwest toward Lily Lake (10,589-foot elevation).

This part of the route continues a gentle ascent and will take you over the North Fork of West Tennessee Creek and around the north side of Lily Lake. Once you're on the north side of Lily Lake, look for a large, open, and flat meadow on your right (north). Continue skiing north, traversing this meadow until you pick up the trail that continues on the north side. The trail veers northeast and then back to the northwest, climbing over a gradual slope with large open glades for more than 1 mile. Watch carefully for the blue diamonds that are used as trail markers on the trees. These blue diamonds will lead you directly north, across Slide Creek, and finally to the 10th Mountain Division Hut.

Detailed topo maps, a compass, and a GPS unit to help navigate your way to the hut are essential. While the terrain is novice to intermediate at best, the greatest challenge is navigating through an area where there are trails in all directions.

Follow the route back to the trailhead. Please remember that the use of the 10th Mountain Hut is for guests with reservations only. Please respect their privacy if you're not staying overnight.

How to get there

From Denver go west on I–70 approximately 105 miles to exit 171 and Minturn. This exit is approximately 5.4 miles west of Vail. At the bottom of the off-ramp, make a right and head south on U.S. Highway 24. Go over the top of Tennessee Pass and proceed another 1.6 miles to the Crane Park turnoff. Watch for signs indicating Forest Road 100.

From Leadville, drive 8.8 miles north on U.S. Highway 24 from the junction of Colorado Highway 91 to the Crane Park turnoff. Parking is limited, and all vehicles must park on the west side of U.S. Highway 24.

Pearl Pass

White River and Gunnison National Forests, Ashcroft to Crested Butte, CO

Type of trail:	▬▬
Distance:	25 miles one way; pick up shuttle vehicle at the end of the trail for the five-hour drive back to Aspen.
Terrain:	Extremely challenging climbs and descents from one end of the trail to the other.
Trail difficulty:	Advanced.
Surface quality:	Ungroomed backcountry conditions along the entire route.
Elevation:	The trail starts at 9,498 feet, climbs to the top of Pearl Pass at 12,705 feet, and ends at the East River trailhead at 8,980 feet.
Time:	2 to 4 full days.
Avalanche danger:	Moderate to extremely high.
Food and facilities:	A lot of advance planning is required for this trip. This is a journey that will tax even the most expert skier and back-country adventurer. It is highly recommended that you consider hiring a guide. Call Aspen Alpine Guides at (970) 925–6618. In Crested Butte call Crested Butte Mountain Guides at (970) 349–5430.

Reservations for the Tagert, Green-Wilson, and Friends Hut must be made in advance. If you have a guide or custom tour, they can take care of those arrangements for you. If you're doing it on your own, you can make reservations and get additional information and brochures by calling the 10th Mountain Division Hut Association at (970) 925–5775.

Groceries, gas, snacks, and drinks are best obtained before leaving the Aspen area. In Aspen you'll find plenty of overnight accommodations with a choice of hotels, motels, bed-and-breakfasts, etc. For further information, call Aspen Central Reservations at (800) 262–7736.

To obtain your free pass to go into Ashcroft Ski Touring Center, contact them at (970) 925–1971. For information about lunch or dinner reservations at Pine Creek Cookhouse, call (970) 925–1044.

I f you ask three different people about this trail, you'll generally get three different opinions on how difficult it is, or how lengthy, or what the snow conditions are like. But this trail from Aspen to Crested Butte via Pearl Pass is a truly classic route that every serious cross-country skier aspires to undertake. It's long. It's technically difficult. It takes you into

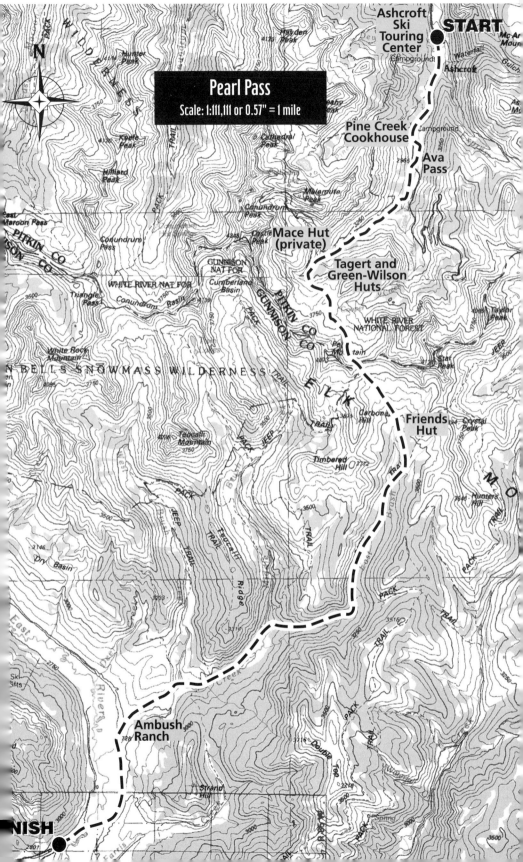

the far reaches of the Elk Mountains. *This is an area where amateurs in map-reading, route finding, avalanche safety, first-aid, and basic winter survival skills should never venture without a guide or an experienced companion.* But for those who are experienced in backcountry skiing and are up to the task, the route rewards them with untold beauty and challenge. This route is a character builder.

In fine weather you can ski it as a two-day trip, but the more practical thing to do, especially after a new snow when you have to break trail yourself, is to plan on staying overnight at both the Tagert and Friends Huts along the way. The Tagert Hut, named for stage driver Billy Tagert, who drove pioneers, hopeful miners, and freight over Taylor Pass during the late 1800s, is located a little over 5 miles from the start of the tour. It makes for a short first day, with two to six hours of skiing, and then a long second day of even more challenging technical skiing.

On the other side of Pearl Pass, you can stay at the Friends Hut. Because of the nature of this route, the strenuous climbs and descents, and the remoteness of the hut, it's best to go with a group of skiers and to reserve the hut for at least two days. *Starting at first light is a must and at least one member of the group must have skied the pass before and possess the skills to find the hut in whiteout conditions.* If you're a first-timer, it is strongly recommended that you hire a professional guide.

This tour starts from Ashcroft Ski Touring Center as so many cross-country outings in this area do. Before starting, visit the center to pick up a free ski pass for the Ava-Pass route. From the trailhead ski south on Castle Creek Road (Forest Road 102) to Pine Creek Cookhouse, and then to avoid dangerous avalanche chutes take the Ava-Pass route, which heads east across Castle Creek. Ski on that for about 0.5 mile, crossing back over the creek to intersect with the main road at the 2-mile point. If the avalanche conditions warrant it, you may be able to follow the road instead of taking the Ava-Pass route. Check ahead with the local avalanche information hotline (970–920–1664) and Ashcroft Ski Touring Center. You'll see a fork in the road. Be sure to take the right—or west—fork, heading south on Castle Creek Road.

Be aware that Castle Creek is laden with avalanche gullies. The trail climbs southwest over two steep inclines, one of which rises about 700 feet in 1 mile, and includes several switchbacks. You'll pass the privately owned Mace Hut and then the cutoff to Montezuma Mine before you veer to the south and ascend steep terrain to Tagert or Green-Wilson Huts at a little over 5.3 miles from the trailhead.

Tagert Hut and Green-Wilson Hut are part of the Alfred Braun Hut System and are available for reservation through the 10th Mountain Division Hut Association. The Tagert Hut sleeps seven people, and the Green-

Directions at a glance

- Park in the parking area near Toklat Lodge. Get a trail pass from Ashcroft Ski Touring Center.

- The trailhead to Pearl Pass leads south along Forest Road 102 from the parking area. Starting at first light is a must.

- Continue on trail approximately 1.5 miles and look for Pine Creek Cookhouse. Good spot for a coffee break, but reservations for lunch and dinner are suggested.

- After Pine Creek Cookhouse, look for the Ava-Pass route, which takes you off the road and down into the Castle Creek area, to avoid known avalanche chutes.

- Ski back on the road at approximately the 2-mile mark.

- The trail will divide. Take the trail to the right and continue to head south and west on Castle Creek Road (Forest Road 102). Be aware of avalanche gullies in Castle Creek. Watch for the privately owned Mace Hut and the cutoff to the Montezuma Mine. From where the trail divides, it's about 3 miles until you see the Tagert and Green-Wilson Huts.

- After your overnight stay, at first light head south on Pearl Pass Road from the huts, staying along Cooper Creek Valley to the top of Pearl Pass. It's about 2.75 miles, but it's steep, and it takes you directly under an avalanche chute.

- At Pearl Pass you'll head southeast for about 1.5 miles to treeline at the upper end of East Brush Creek Valley and east of Carbonate Hill.

- At East Brush Creek, climb past the northwest fork and stop for the night at Friends Hut. The hut is at treeline east of the main drainage.

- Head south from Friends Hut for approximately 0.75 mile. Veer to the southwest and continue down along the trail for approximately 5 miles.

- Traverse west and southwest under Teocalli Ridge and continue southwest another 4 miles to Ambush Ranch.

- Continue southwest into East River Valley along the main four-wheel-drive road. At another 3 miles, pass Cold Spring Ranch, then you'll come to the East River trailhead.

- Pick up your shuttle vehicles. It's a ten-minute drive to Crested Butte and about a five-hour winter drive back to Aspen.

There are great views on the way over Pearl Pass.

Wilson Hut sleeps eight people. These huts have recently been remodeled, and upgraded sleeping, cooking, and latrine facilities have been added. Both huts require a four-person minimum and are rented only to one group at a time—hence the minimum number of overnight guests—and cost $25 per person, per night.

After a good night's sleep, start at first light from the Tagert or Green-Wilson Huts and travel to Pearl Pass by way of Pearl Pass Road. Due to changing weather conditions much of this part of the tour is trekked over the path of least resistance. Basically you head south, staying to the east side of the Pearl Pass basin, climbing and descending severe grades above treeline along Cooper Creek Valley to the pass. The slope on the north side of the pass is the trickiest and takes you directly under an avalanche chute. Mountaineering skills are a must. For the last few hundred feet, you'll climb up one person at a time—standard avalanche precaution. That way if the chute lets loose, only one person will be caught in the slide and the rest can effect a rescue.

After crossing over the pass, follow Pearl Pass Road for about 100 yards before skiing down the short headwall of the valley. Then descend by following the shallow bench that falls off to skier's left. When the bench ends in the main drainage, the hut can be found at treeline on the left or east side of the valley. It's about a 4.5-mile trek from the Tagert and Green-Wilson Huts to Friends Hut. But don't let the relatively short distance fool you. It's going to take you a good three to six hours of hard skiing if the weather conditions are anything but ideal.

Built in honor of ten people who were killed in a midair collision over East Maroon Pass, the Friends Hut has given shelter to many a skier venturing over the pass since 1985. As do most huts, it contains a wood stove, a propane cookstove, firewood, cookware, mattresses, and dishes. Light is supplied by a photovoltaic system, and water is obtained by melting snow. No dogs are allowed. The cost is $25 per person, per night, and eight people can sleep comfortably. More than one group can be booked at a time, so if you want the cabin to yourselves, you can reserve it for $100 per night.

The second half of the route from Friends Hut to the East River trailhead near Crested Butte begins through the thick stands of trees, heading south. Descend along a creek bed for approximately 0.75 mile, then veer to the southwest, eventually arriving in the Brush Creek drainage just under 6 miles from Friends Hut. If snow conditions are right, stay with the four-wheel-drive trail and head southwest over the open valley bottom, then traverse west and southwest across the south rim of Teocalli Ridge.

Stay on the trail, heading southwest to intersect with another trail. Keep heading southwest until you pass Ambush Ranch. Not much to see here, but the fences and pens will give you a good bearing, and you'll be able to note that you've now gone just over 10 miles for the day—luckily most of it has been downhill. Just past Ambush Ranch is the junction of the Brush Creek and East River Valleys. It is a dirt road in the summer but can be covered with snow in the winter. Head south over a valley that mercifully is pretty level to Cold Spring Ranch. Just a little farther ahead to the southwest is the East River trailhead. Here is where you pick up your shuttle cars for the ten-minute drive to Crested Butte and nearly five-hour drive back to Aspen.

How to get there

From Aspen go west on Colorado Highway 82 approximately 0.75 mile. From the roundabout take Castle Creek Road past the hospital. It's also marked as Forest Road 102. Drive on the winding Castle Creek Road for approximately 11.5 miles and park near Toklat Lodge at the lot marked for the trail on the left, or east, side of the road. The parking area is pretty large, so finding a spot is usually not a problem for either day or overnight parking.

Lindley Hut

White River National Forest, Ashcroft, CO

Type of trail:	
Distance:	8 miles.
Terrain:	Easy to moderate climbs and descents from one end of the trail to the other.
Trail difficulty:	Novice to intermediate.
Surface quality:	Ungroomed, but sometimes tracked by skiers or snowshoers.
Elevation:	The trail starts at 9,498 feet and ends at 10,624 feet at Lindley Hut.
Time:	3 to 5 hours.
Snowmobile use:	Low.
Avalanche danger:	Extreme potential for avalanches exists along the trail.
Food and facilities:	If you're planning on staying overnight at Lindley Hut, advance reservations are required. Additional information and brochures can be obtained by calling the 10th Mountain Division Hut Association at (970) 925–5775. The hut opens for overnight guests around Thanksgiving but requires a minimum of eight people in a group for reservations.

Groceries, gas, snacks, and drinks are best obtained before leaving the Aspen area. In Aspen you'll find plenty of overnight accommodations with a choice of hotels, motels, bed-and-breakfasts, etc. For further information, call Aspen Central Reservations at (800) 262–7736.

To obtain your free pass to use the Ava-Pass route, contact Ashcroft Ski Touring Center at (970) 925–1971. Following the direct route up the county road doesn't require a pass. For information about lunch or dinner reservations at Pine Creek Cookhouse, call (970) 925–1044. For guides and customized tours, call Aspen Alpine Guides at (970) 925–6618. For equipment rentals and repairs call Aspen Cross-Country Center at (970) 925–2145 or Ute Mountaineers at (970) 925–2849.

Located in the spectacularly rugged Elk Mountains, the trails stemming from the Aspen area enter into remote and difficult terrain where skills of route finding and avalanche safety and intermediate skiing ability are a must. The trail to Lindley Hut is technically one of the easier trails in this area. The first half of the route is relatively flat and well marked to avoid dangerous avalanche chutes. The second half of the

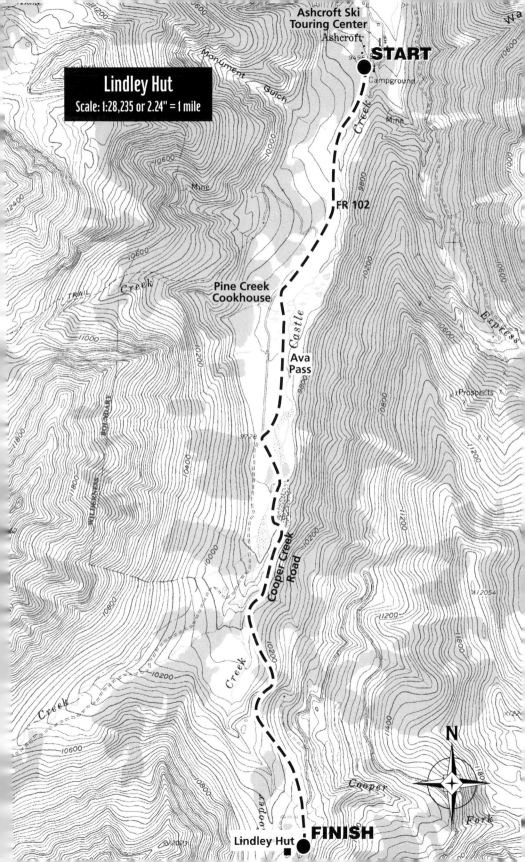

Getting ready for the big trek.

trail follows a road offering a climb that snowshoers will enjoy and skiers will have to work at. The trail leaves the road sometime during the second half and some route finding will be necessary.

Lindley Hut is actually the largest in the Alfred Braun Hut System and can accommodate up to fourteen people. Like most huts it offers a wood-burning stove for heat. Water is obtained by melting snow. During the summer of 2002, the hut was remodeled and new sleeping, cooking, and latrine facilities were added. Because the area is so isolated and skiers or snowshoers can easily trigger avalanches, a minimum of eight people are required to reserve the hut overnight for safety reasons.

Before you start your tour, you need to get a trail pass at Ashcroft Ski Touring Center. From the trailhead at the center, ski or snowshoe south on Castle Creek Road—also marked as Forest Road 102—over a couple of moderate hills to Pine Creek Cookhouse at about 1.5 miles from the trailhead. Pine Creek Cookhouse is a good spot for lunch and dinner, but it's often crowded, so advance reservations are suggested. You normally can stop off and at least get a cup of hot chocolate or coffee while en route.

After Pine Creek Cookhouse, you'll see a lot of signs warning of avalanche danger, and reach an Ava-Pass Trail intersection where you may leave the road. If conditions warrant head east across Castle Creek before bending back around to the south to intersect with the road again at the 2-mile point. Ava-Pass Trail is well marked and takes you out of the paths of known chutes.

Once you get back on the road, look for the trail to fork. The trail to the right leads farther up Castle Creek and is the route for advanced skiers who are heading up over Pearl Pass. If you are on your way to Lindley Hut, you will want the east or left fork, which is Cooper Creek Road; head south. Steadily climb up for 1.75 miles, winding in and out of the trees. On the left will be slopes with a potential for avalanches, so take extreme care. Avalanche beacons and snow shovels should be part of your standard equipment.

Directions at a glance

- Park in the parking area near Toklat Lodge. Get a free trail pass from Ashcroft Ski Touring Center.
- The trail to Lindley Hut leads south along Forest Road 102 from the parking area.
- Continue on the trail approximately 1.5 miles and look for Pine Creek Cookhouse. Good spot for a coffee break. Reservations for lunch and dinner are suggested.
- After Pine Creek Cookhouse, look for the Ava-Pass route that takes you off the road and down into the Castle Creek area. This trail avoids known avalanche chutes. If the avalanche danger is low follow the more direct route on the road.
- Ski back on the road at approximately the 2-mile mark. Look for the fork in the trail. Take the trail to the east—or left—and follow Cooper Creek Road.
- Climb steadily for the next 1.75 miles. Be aware that avalanche danger does exist.
- When the trail breaks into open area on top and the road switches back to the north, leave the trail and head down (south) 0.13 mile to Lindley Hut.
- To return to the trailhead, take the same route back down.

When the terrain levels at the top of the last rise and the road U-turns to the north, it's time to leave the road and head south for the last 0.13 mile to Lindley Hut. The hut lies near the creek and behind a dense grove of spruce trees.

To return to the trailhead, take the same route back and enjoy the gentle downhill glide or trek.

How to get there

From Aspen go west on Colorado Highway 82 approximately 0.75 mile. From the roundabout take Castle Creek Road past the hospital. It's also marked as Forest Road 102. Drive on the winding Castle Creek Road for approximately 11.5 miles and park near Toklat Lodge at the lot marked for the trail on the left, or east, side of the road. The parking area is pretty large, so finding a spot is usually not a problem for either day or overnight parking.

Babbish Gulch

White River National Forest, Glenwood Springs, CO

Type of trail:	▬▬ ⬤
Also used by:	Some downhill skiers and snowboarders.
Distance:	Lower Trail Loop—10 miles; Lower and Upper Meadows Trail Loops combined—18 miles.
Terrain:	Easy and gradual for the first several miles. Then moderate climbs and descents throughout Lower Trail Loop.
Trail difficulty:	Intermediate.
Surface quality:	Lower Trail Loop is groomed and maintained by Sunlight Mountain Resort. Upper Meadows Trail Loop is ungroomed but often tracked by skiers or snowshoers.
Elevation:	The trailhead is at 7,800 feet, and you will climb to 9,600 feet.
Time:	3 hours to full day.
Avalanche danger:	Low.
Food and facilities:	The trail is located close to Glenwood Springs, where there are many fine restaurants, lounges, grocery stores, and overnight accommodations. It's also located at the base of Sunlight Mountain Resort, so there are plenty of rooms, condos, and restaurants conveniently located at the starting and stopping point of the trail. For complete snowshoeing or ski information, call Sunlight Mountain Resort (800–445–7931). Additional overnight accommodations can be made at the resort area through Sunlight Mountain Inn (800–733–4757) and Brettelberg Inn (800–634–0481).

While Sunlight Mountain Resort has four chair lifts for downhill skiing and charges a daily fee, they also maintain just over 10 miles of backcountry cross-country ski and snowshoe trails that are available to everyone at no charge. The trailhead is located at the resort, and Lower Trail Loop is groomed and maintained throughout the season. The 10-mile loop is rated as intermediate. The trail runs to the east for the first 0.5 mile along the relatively flat Old Fourmile Road, which turns into Williams (Road) Trail. Here is where it becomes steeper and starts climbing uphill to the south. The loop follows a summertime horseback and llama path and is a combination of moderate up- and downhill climbs with a wide, well-marked trail surrounded by groves of aspen and pine trees. You'll see plenty of tree squirrels and even an occasional blue grouse along the trail. The tree stands are thick and mature, providing a

good windbreak even when the weather is blustery. A lot of smaller ungroomed and unmarked trails inside this main loop cut diagonally off the main trail if you're looking for shortcuts that are not crowded!

Approximately 5 miles up Williams Trail is a small warming hut and rest area. There are no facilities here, but it's a good opportunity to take a break at this halfway point. Get out of the weather and off the trail, sit inside on the hardwood floor, and enjoy a sack lunch. The trail divides at this warming hut and offers three options. You can follow the markers that connect with Dipsy Doodle Trail to the northeast. This trail will continue the loop back down the mountain and bring you back to the Sunlight/Fourmile trailhead. The second option is to take the groomed trail that traverses the mountain to the east and intersects with the resort's downhill ski area, called the Ute Downhill Run. Your last option is to

Directions at a glance

- Trail routes begin at the edge of the Sunlight Mountain Resort parking lot to the east. At 0.25 mile there is a rustic cabin along the Fourmile Road. Continue past the cabin another 0.25 mile to Williams Trail.
- Trail heads south and climbs up through conifers and aspen trees.
- At top of trail, at approximately 5 miles, there is a warming hut for a rest stop and lunch. No facilities here.
- From the warming hut follow the marked trail northeast and intersect the marked Dipsy Doodle Trail. Head downhill on it back to the Sunlight/Babbish Gulch trailhead.

Alternate route 1

- Ski or snowshoe east from the warming hut and intersect the downhill ski run.
- Ski or snowshoe down the ski run to return to the trailhead at Sunlight Mountain Resort.

Alternate route 2

- From the warming hut continue south to the higher Upper Meadows Trail.
- These trails are ungroomed and provide backcountry trailblazing opportunities.
- Trails all loop back down to the warming hut. Take Dipsy Doodle trail from the warming hut back downhill to trailhead.

continue from the warming hut, going higher on the Upper Meadows Trail, which allows you to head into the backcountry on ungroomed snow.

This additional 8-mile Upper Meadows loop is also rated as intermediate, but it provides a more challenging backcountry experience because you may need to break your own trail and will be traveling less-used terrain. Upper Meadows loop begins and ends at the warming hut, from which you will enjoy a mostly downhill glide on groomed snow back to the trailhead after an afternoon of trailblazing.

Approximately 0.25 mile to the east from the trailhead, located alongside Old Fourmile Road, is a rustic cabin that can be rented on a nightly basis from the resort. The cost is $40 per night for your entire group. The cabin will sleep up to six people, and at $40 per night for everyone, this is a real backcountry bargain. The resort provides firewood for heating and cooking as well as electricity. An outhouse is nearby, and you have to provide all of your own sleeping bags, cooking gear, etc. If you're looking for more civilized accommodations, Sunlight Mountain Inn has bed-and-breakfast style lodging, while Brettelberg Inn offers a host of condominiums.

How to get there

From Glenwood Springs take Grand Avenue south from I–70 to Fourmile Road and proceed about 10 miles to Sunlight Mountain Resort . The trailhead is on the west end of the parking lot at the base of the area. There is plenty of parking in the lot. Fourmile Road continues past the ski area, but snowmobiles are allowed there.

West Bench Trail

Grand Mesa National Forest, Grand Junction, CO

Type of trail:	▬▬ ⬤
Distance:	7 to 12 miles.
Terrain:	Gradual climbs all along the trail ridge, and great downhill runs to Powderhorn Resort.
Trail difficulty:	Intermediate.
Surface quality:	Ungroomed, but usually tracked by skiers or snowshoers along the trail and ridgeline. Packed and groomed downhill runs at the ski resort.
Elevation:	The trailhead is at 9,870 feet to the ridge above Powderhorn Resort at 9,700 feet.
Time:	3 hours to full day.
Avalanche danger:	Low.
Food and facilities:	Mesa Lakes Resort is open year-round and serves winter users. Downhill, cross-country, and snowshoe equipment, clothing, and accessories are available through their rental ski shop. For overnight information or a brochure on their facilities, call Mesa Lakes Resort at (970) 268–5467. Gas, groceries, restaurants, and a liquor store are located 14 miles back up Colorado Highway 65 in Mesa. At Powderhorn Resort you'll also find overnight accommodations, restaurants, and lounges. For a brochure and more information about Powderhorn Resort, call them at (970) 268–5700. For more information about cross-country skiing and snowshoeing in the area, contact the Grand Mesa Nordic Council at (970) 434–9753, or visit the Web site at outdoors.at/gmuc.

The Grand Mesa region is a mecca for snowmobilers, cross-country skiers, and snowshoers. Literally hundreds of miles of trails run all across this giant flat-top mountain. Many of these trails are shared by all types of winter enthusiasts, and they are often very crowded, so solitude is rare. However, there are several areas where snowmobiles are not allowed. Some of these trail networks, such as Skyway, County Line, and Ward Lake have groomed trails for nordic skiers and snowshoers. In fact, cross-country skiers and snowshoers account for more visits to Grand Mesa than snowmobilers. The Grand Mesa Nordic Council maintains the trail systems and can provide information about them. The maintained trail systems attract 8,000 to 10,000 skiers every year.

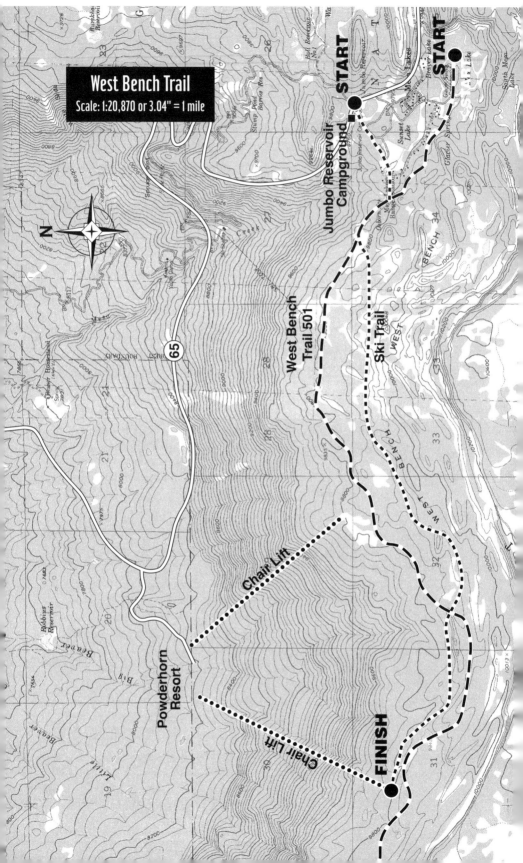

There are also some excellent unmaintained backcountry trails on Grand Mesa. The most popular is West Bench Trail 501. About an hour from Grand Junction is a scenic area with plenty of activities available; and no snowmobile traffic is allowed to compete for the trail. The trail that begins at Mesa Lakes Resort is rated for intermediate skiers and snowshoers. West Bench Trail is a ridgeline route with a nearly constant series of small to moderate rolling hills. The trail is marked with both Forest Service tree patches and occasional signage.

Most people park at the Jumbo Reservoir Campground parking lot about 0.25 mile from Mesa Lakes Resort. But you will find a trailhead for Trail 501 at either place.

Stay along the top of the ridge, and the trail will take you through small breaks that are lined with groves of aspen and spruce trees. When the weather turns blustery, the trees provide an excellent windbreak, and blowing snow across the path is minimal. Approximately 3.5 miles from the trailhead, the path opens up and climbs gently to the top of chair lift 1 at Powderhorn Resort. Here snowshoers, cross-country skiers, or tele-markers can check in with the lift operators and receive a "token" that enables them to ski or snowshoe down to Powderhorn Resort for lunch and a little rest and relaxation. Then they can ride the lift back up for free!

Directions at a glance

- The West Bench trailhead begins in the parking lot of Mesa Lakes Resort and is marked Trail 501.
- Stay along the top of the ridge, head west, and watch for occasional Forest Service wooden signs and tree patches.
- Continue along the ridgeline west for approximately 3.5 miles and look for the top of Powderhorn Resort chair lift 1. Get a "token" from the lift operators and ski to base for lunch.
- Return route is by riding the chair lift back up the mountain and following the trail back to Mesa Lakes Resort.

Alternate route

- If you don't want to go down chair lift 1, continue on West Bench Trail heading west for another 2.5 miles to chair lift 2.
- Get a token from the lift operator and ski down to base of Powderhorn Resort for lunch, or turn around and ski or trek approximately 6 miles back to the trailhead at Mesa Lakes Resort.

If you're not ready to head down to the ski resort, continue on West Bench Trail, which continues to follow the ridgeline. The trail is still good for intermediate skiers and is for the most part pretty flat. It's an area that's good for level to mild rolling ridges, gentle snowshoeing, and glide skiing. Ahead 2.5 miles is the top of chair lift 2 at Powderhorn Resort. Once again check in with the lift operators and secure your free token before heading down the hill.

If you want to start at Powderhorn Resort, a one-trip "up the lift" pass will cost $10. Although many of the ski areas in Colorado will let cross-country skiers and snowshoers use their resort runs to come down from higher elevations, many have restrictions about allowing this kind of winter sports recreation to start on the commercial downhill chair lifts. Powderhorn Resort is one that welcomes all outdoor winter recreationalists. At the top of either chair lift 1 or 2, you can ski back along the ridge on the West Bench Trail to the trailhead at Mesa Lakes Resort.

At Mesa Lakes Resort, parking and access to all of the cross-country ski and snowshoe trails are free. Overnight accommodations at the resort begin at $45 for a motel room and go up to $150 for cabins that will sleep up to twelve people. The main lodge burned down during the winter of 2002. Plans were made to rebuild it during the summer. Be sure to call ahead to make sure lodging is available.

How to get there

From Grand Junction take I–70 east approximately 12 miles to Colorado Highway 65. Head toward Powderhorn Resort. Stay on Colorado Highway 65 for approximately 25 miles to the Jumbo Reservoir Campground parking lot about 0.25 mile from Mesa Lakes Resort. There is some parking near the resort but it is limited. This is approximately 4.5 miles after passing Powderhorn Resort. The trailhead for West Bench Trail begins at the edge of Mesa Lakes Resort and is well marked.

Old Monarch Pass

San Isabel and Gunnison National Forests, Salida, CO

Type of trail:	━━━ 🌟
Also used by:	Snowmobilers.
Distance:	3 miles to 21 miles, depending on trail chosen.
Terrain:	Gradual climb at the beginning, and great downhill runs and trails down to where you leave the shuttle car.
Trail difficulty:	Intermediate to advanced, depending on trail chosen.
Surface quality:	Ungroomed, but usually well tracked by skiers.
Elevation:	The trailhead is at 10,950 feet; Old Monarch Pass, 11,373 feet; and the end of trail on Major Creek 9,550 feet.
Time:	2 hours to all day.
Avalanche danger:	Low to moderate.
Snowmobile use:	Moderate to heavy, depending on trail chosen.
Food and facilities:	Use restaurant and gas facilities before leaving Salida. At the Monarch Ski and Snowboard Resort there is a restaurant, bar, and cafeteria open to the public. The Monarch Mountain Lodge, about 4.5 miles back down the hill from the ski slopes, has nice modern rooms, very reasonable rates, and a great restaurant and bar in which to unwind. For package information call (800) 332–3668. For information about lodging in Salida, call the Salida Chamber of Commerce at (877) 772–5432.

Old Monarch Pass offers great snow conditions and an opportunity to practice every sort of skiing or snowshoeing. If you only want to ski for half a day, just head out from the trailhead for 1.5 miles to the top of Old Monarch Pass. You'll see an open park that's great for mastering flat-track techniques. The trail is rated easy to moderate and lined with giant pines and conifer trees. If you want to try out powder or cut some telemark turns, head up the small peak to the south of the old pass and carve your way down to the park.

For those who might want the challenge of an all-day tour, just continue down the west side of the pass for 9 miles of gliding or downhill snowshoeing above No Name Creek. At the bottom, you'll be glad to see the shuttle vehicle you parked there to save the long haul back up the hill.

Because you're skiing or snowshoeing on the east side of Old Monarch Pass as you begin, you'll be skiing right next to the Monarch Ski and Snowboard Resort. It's marked with a boundary rope, and speeding

Old Monarch Pass

Scale: 1:62,500 or 1.01" = 1 mile

Campground

Deadman

Creek

No Name

Monarch
Ski and
Snowboard
Resort

Lifts

STA

FINISH

2712

Major

Creek

Porphyry

Creek

2974

3000

Powerline

North Fork

36

2715

Creek

Highway 50

3609

2760

Campground

Tomichi Creek

White Pine
Turnoff

N

Testing out the ski legs.

downhill skiers will often cruise right past you. This happens only for a short section of the trail, and as long as both groups stay on their sides of the rope, there shouldn't be any trouble.

One of the fun things about this trail is its history, dating back to 1879 when it was used by mountain travelers and miners in search of gold. In truth the trail was in use for hundreds of years before that by the Ute Indians, who lived in, hunted, and traveled these mountains. Another fun thing about this trip is the incredible view from the top of Old Monarch Pass.

From the top of Old Monarch Pass, where you will cross the Continental Divide, the road traverses a steep slope to the right going northwest until it crosses over the ridge between Porphyry Creek and Major Creek. Then it winds down the north side of that ridge until it arrives in Pitkin. All along the way there are great views of Tomichi Creek Valley.

How to get there

From Salida drive approximately 18 miles west on U.S. Highway 50 toward Gunnison. Go past the Monarch Ski Resort for approximately 0.7 mile and look for a highway sign on your right that reads OLD MONARCH PASS. The parking area at the trailhead is usually plowed and provides parking for twelve to fifteen vehicles.

To get your shuttle vehicle to the end of the route, go 8.8 miles west from the trailhead parking area over Old Monarch Pass on U.S. Highway

Directions at a glance

- From the trailhead parking area, begin a gradual ascent up the Old Monarch Pass road.

- Approximately 1.5 miles from the trailhead, the route opens up into a meadow park. Numerous small clearings are available to trek or ski through. Ski back to the car following the same route if you don't plan to ski over the pass.

- If you are going on, the road traverses a steep hill to the right of the top of the pass and crosses the ridge between Porphyry Creek and Major Creek, then winds down to where you parked the car at the snow closure. The road slopes gently all the way.

50. On the western side of the pass, look for White Pine Road on the Gunnison–Saguache county line. Make a right and go north on White Pine Road for 4.7 miles. Then get on Old Monarch Pass road heading east until you hit the snow closure. Parking here is sparse. When you leave your vehicle, park it so others can get around. Reverse the trip back up to Old Monarch Pass and start skiing or snowshoeing.

Washington Gulch to Elkton Cabins

Gunnison National Forest, Crested Butte, CO

Type of trail:	▬▬ ▦
Also used by:	Snowmobilers.
Distance:	11 miles.
Terrain:	Level to rolling with gradual climbs to the cabins.
Trail difficulty:	Novice to intermediate.
Surface quality:	Ungroomed, but usually well tracked by skiers, snowshoers, and snowmobilers.
Elevation:	The trailhead is at 9,450 feet; Elkton Cabins are at 10,700 feet; elevation gain moderate, averaging about 200 feet per mile.
Time:	3 to 5 hours.
Avalanche danger:	Low.
Snowmobile use:	Medium.
Food and facilities:	Food, gas, equipment, and a number of fine restaurants can be found in Crested Butte. If you need to stay overnight before heading to the hut, there are also plenty of accommodations in Crested Butte and at the base of the ski area. For information about lodging call the Crested Butte Chamber of Commerce at (800) 545–4505 or visit www.crestedbuttechamber.com. For more information on Crested Butte trails, contact Crested Butte Nordic Center (970–349–1707); to reserve one of the huts, call at (970) 349–1815. For guide services call Crested Butte Guides at (970) 349–5430.

Surrounded by the majestic vistas of the Elk Mountains and the Ruby–Anthracite Range, Crested Butte is a haven for nordic skiers and is thought by many to be the birthplace of the modern American telemark turn. Over the same routes used by mountain bikers during the summer, winter outdoor enthusiasts can explore the vast backcountry famous for its beauty, accessibility, and ruggedness. There are also a number of huts in the area that can serve as excellent base camps for backcountry adventure. The three huts in the old mining townsite of Elkton—Elkton Cabin, Miner's Delight, and Mosquito Hut—are examples.

The trail to the abandoned mining camp of Elkton is a well-established, popular route shared by snowmobilers, snowshoers, and backcountry skiers. The best time to go is after a fresh snow when you can break trail yourself and enjoy the calm and peace of the gently rolling terrain.

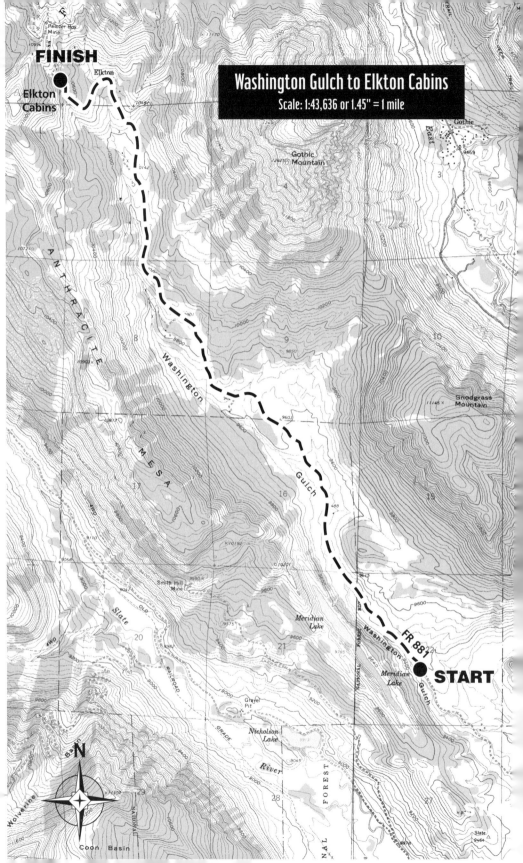

FINISH

Elkton Cabins

Elkton

Washington Gulch to Elkton Cabins
Scale: 1:43,636 or 1.45" = 1 mile

Gothic

Gothic Mountain

ANTHRACITE

Washington

MESA

Gulch

Snodgrass Mountain

Smith Hill Mine

Meridian Lake

Slate

OLD RAILROAD

Washington Gulch

FR 881

Meridian Lake

START

Gravel Pit

Nicholson Lake

GRACE

River

NATIONAL FOREST

N

Wolverine

Coon Basin

From the parking area and trailhead signs (Forest Road 811), you ski or snowshoe up the valley over level to rolling terrain that's ideal for the beginner and intermediate skier or snowshoer. After touring the easy-to-follow Washington Gulch Road, you'll come to a sustained climb at the 6-mile road sign near the southwest corner of Gothic Mountain. Once past this section, the road climbs gradually, passing below the mountain's southwest face. From here, the terrain becomes increasingly steep as you cross the mouth of a drainage to the northeast, then turn west (left) and south (left) across a creek and the head of Washington Gulch.

After crossing the creek, make the final climb to Elkton by ascending a switchback, heading northwest. When you arrive, you'll see two cabins off to the right. The first cabin, the one closest to the road, is Elkton Cabin. Originally a miner's cabin built in the 1860s, it was the first of the three cabins to be made into a ski hut. With a wood-burning stove for heat, a gas stove for cooking, cooking gear, sheets and blankets, an outhouse, and directions to a nearby water supply, this cabin makes a convenient base camp for a day trip, but reservations are required. All you'll have to carry in is your food. The Elkton Cabin sleeps six people.

The other two cabins, Miner's Delight and Mosquito Hut, offer the same amenities. Miner's Delight sleeps twelve and Mosquito Hut sleeps six. The owners of the huts will also provide food and cook for you if requested. A fourth cabin, called the Silver Jewell, is in the works and will feature hot water, with a shower, a stereo, and an oven, all powered by solar cells.

While you're there, spend the day hiking, skiing, and exploring the area that was famous in the late 1880s and early 1990s for its mining operations. There is also great skiing in the bowl to the east of Baldy Mountain. Although snowmobiles are permitted in the area, they are strongly discouraged near the huts, so you should have a quiet stay. If you're not staying overnight at Elkton Cabin, it's a nice gentle glide or trek back down the same route to the trailhead.

How to get there

The well-marked trailhead is at the end of a county road near the Meridian Lake Development. From the stop sign at the intersection of Elk Avenue and County Road 317 in Crested Butte (Colorado Highway 135 turns into County Road 317), drive north for 1.7 miles to the Washington Gulch and Meridian Lake turnoff. Turn left onto Washington Gulch Road (Forest Road 811) and proceed along the main road to the plowed parking area at the winter road closure.

Rainbow Lake

Gunnison National Forest, Gunnison, CO

Type of trail:	▬ ☷ ◁
Also used by:	Snowmobilers.
Distance:	22 miles.
Terrain:	Level road with lots of rolling gentle hills.
Trail difficulty:	Novice.
Surface quality:	Ungroomed, but sometimes tracked by skiers, snowshoers, and snowmobilers.
Elevation:	The trailhead is at 7,600 feet, and you will climb to 10,900 feet at Rainbow Lake.
Time:	4 hours to full day.
Avalanche danger:	Low.
Snowmobile use:	Low.
Food and facilities:	Rainbow Lake Road is located about 13 miles west of Gunnison, which has many fine restaurants, overnight accommodations, grocery stores, etc. Fill up your car with gas and get all of your snacks, lunches, and drinks before leaving town. For information about dining and lodging in Gunnison, call the Gunnison Country Chamber of Commerce at (970) 641–1000 or visit www.gunnison-co.com.

Rainbow Lake Road has a very extreme southern exposure. Because of this, light snows often melt quickly. If the area has a heavy snow and snow pack, it is an excellent and scenic trail from around Christmas until early April. If the snow is sparse, the trail can be spotty and even muddy, especially in the late spring. Mid- to late winter months are by far the best for using this uncrowded trail.

Beginning at the snow closure gate, Rainbow Lake Road climbs very gently and steadily up through wide-open sagebrush country into a small canyon that follows the East Fork of Dry Creek. Small groves of aspen trees mark your ascent. As the canyon narrows, prehistoric rock pillars dot the landscape above you, and there are leftover, eroded mud columns that date back nearly one hundred million years. In eons past the area was covered with boiling hot mud from a nearby volcano. Much of it has eroded away, but spires are still left as remnants. The very unusual geologic formations provide great photo opportunities.

Elevation increases are gradual on Rainbow Lake Road, but there are a lot of rolling hills. These ridges continue all the way up to Rainbow

Lake where the terrain changes from sagebrush and aspen tree groves to conifer stands. The trail follows Dry Creek through all of these different ecosystems. In truth it is anything but dry and is replete with countless small beaver ponds, dams, and huts.

Lower elevations—the first 2 to 5 miles—are favorite wintering grounds for hundreds of resident deer and elk. Wildlife viewing opportunities are fantastic. A good set of binoculars and a camera with lots of film should be considered musts in everyone's standard equipment.

One of the nice features about this trail is that you can turn around and go back just about anywhere along the route that's convenient or comfortable. Simply turn around and enjoy the gentle hills and gradual descent back to the trailhead.

Once you get back to your parked vehicle, you may be interested in the frozen Blue Mesa Reservoir across U.S. Highway 50. You may enjoy walking downhill less than 0.25 mile to the lake and practicing skate skiing, flatland snowshoeing, and even a little ice fishing! When Blue Mesa Reservoir is frozen, it provides nearly 100 miles of totally uncrowded shoreline for skate skiing, snowshoeing, and angling. Many winter enthusiasts ski or snowshoe out on the lake early in the morning, drill a few holes, and do a little through-the-ice fishing for rainbows, brown trout, lake trout, and Kokanee salmon. Then after an early morning of angling, skate skiing, or snowshoeing, it's time to begin a scenic midmorning journey back up along Rainbow Lake Road.

Directions at a glance

- Trailhead begins at the road closure sign and is marked Forest Road 724.

- Trail makes a gentle ascent and goes along the East Fork of Dry Creek.

- Trail continues on Forest Road 724 for just over 11 miles with lots of small up- and downhill ridges.

- To return trek or ski back very gentle downhill slopes and ridges to trailhead.

How to get there

From the city of Gunnison head west on U.S. Highway 50 approximately 13 miles to the Rainbow Lake Road turnoff. The road is well marked with Park Service signs. The turnout for Rainbow Lake Road will be on your right. Park Service/Forest Service road closure signs are located less than 0.25 mile from U.S. Highway 50. Although the area is open to snowmobiles, because of snow closure signs, snowmobile use is very low.

Lottis Creek

Gunnison National Forest, Taylor Canyon, CO

Type of trail:	━━━ ••••
Distance:	12.2 miles.
Terrain:	Steady climbs to the trail's end and then a fast glide or trek back to the trailhead.
Trail difficulty:	Novice to intermediate.
Surface quality:	Ungroomed, but sometimes tracked by skiers and snowshoers.
Elevation:	The trailhead is at 9,250 feet at Lottis Creek Campground, and you will ascend to above 10,716 feet.
Time:	4 hours to full day.
Avalanche danger:	Low for first 3.4 miles; increases to moderate after that.
Food and facilities:	No facilities are found during the winter at Lottis Creek Trail. There are plenty of restaurants, hotels, and grocery stores in Gunnison, less than 30 miles away. Seventeen miles back down the canyon at Almont, where County Road 742 cuts off from Colorado Highway 135, you'll find the Three Rivers Resort and Outfitters (970–641–1303). Snacks, some dry goods, and gas are available, as are some winter cabins. You'll also find Almont Resort (970–641–4009), with a restaurant and bar open for breakfast, lunch, and dinner. Sack lunches are also available with generous portions.

Approximately 13 miles farther up Taylor Canyon from the Lottis Creek trailhead, you'll discover the Taylor Reservoir area where there are even more cross-country ski and snowshoe trails that start at the Taylor Park Trading Post (970–641–2555). Gas and dry goods only are available during the winter at this popular summer resort area.

The trail begins approximately 0.1 mile above the campground area on County Road 742. The trailhead is well marked as Trail 428. There is a warning to visitors that the area is not open to motorized vehicles because it heads into a designated wilderness area. The trail heads southeast and up into the Fossil Ridge Wilderness Area. Approximately 0.75 mile from trailhead, the trail divides. The left fork, which heads east, is a route that is designated as Trail 758. This trail will lead you into the Union Canyon area. Although popular with summer hikers and campers, the area often has high avalanche danger. It's a 2.5-mile trail that should be avoided unless you've checked and been advised that the avalanche danger is low!

START

Lottis Creek
Campground

Rd 742

Frozen
Waterfalls

South

TR 428

Lottis

Creek

Lottis Creek
Scale: 1:36,923 or 1.72" = 1 mile

Frozen
Waterfalls

South

Lottis

Creek

Cross
Mtn

N

Creek

FINISH

Trailers can be a good way to haul whatever you need.

To continue on South Lottis Creek, take the right fork and stay on Trail 428. This trail heads in a more southerly direction and meanders gently along the creek. On some maps it's also called Gunsight Trail, a name locals also use for it because it leads to Gunsight Pass. The trail crosses the creek, and there are small- to medium-sized waterfalls that are usually frozen solid and make for spectacular cascading ice sculptures and photo opportunities.

This trail begins gently but as it—and you—climb steadily uphill, it becomes steeper. Skiers and snowshoers start at a narrow creek that climbs gently up into a broad but forested valley loaded with stands of conifers and aspen trees.

About 6 miles from the trailhead, you'll have climbed more than 1,400 feet in elevation. Even though the ele-

Directions at a glance

- The trailhead is marked as Trail 428. Head southeast from the campground.

- At about 0.75 mile look for Trail 758 that cuts off to the left and goes east.

- Continue steady climbing along Trail 428, which runs parallel to South Lottis Creek.

- The trail continues a gentle climb for another 5 miles.

- To return go back on the same trail and enjoy the gentle downhill snowshoeing or skiing to the trailhead.

vation increase is pretty large, this trail is a favorite for folks looking for a gentle but continuous climb. It's an easy walk back downhill if you're on snowshoes and a fast glide back down to the trailhead if you're on skis.

How to get there

From Gunnison go north on Colorado Highway 135 approximately 10 miles to the town of Almont. At Almont, make a right on County Road 742 up through Taylor Canyon, approximately 17 miles to Lottis Creek Campground. The parking area is small, but it's usually plowed and open during most of the winter.

Waunita Pass

Gunnison National Forest, Gunnison, CO

Type of trail:	▬▬ ⬭
Also used by:	Snowmobilers.
Distance:	16 miles.
Terrain:	Steady climbs along forest roads to the top of pass for novices. More challenging and steeper ascents along the intermediate route.
Trail difficulty:	Novice to intermediate (difficult trails are also available).
Surface quality:	Ungroomed, but often tracked by skiers, snowshoers, and snowmobilers.
Elevation:	The trailhead is at 8,990 feet at Waunita Hot Springs Ranch, and you will climb to 10,300 feet at Waunita Pass.
Time:	3 to 5 hours.
Avalanche danger:	Low.
Snowmobile use:	Medium.
Food and facilities:	Gunnison lies about 25 miles south and west. The closest hotel and restaurant facilities are about 1 mile east of Gunnison in Tomichi Village. Call (970) 641–1131 for reservations at the Tomichi Village Best Western Hotel. Many other fine restaurants, overnight accommodations, grocery stores, etc. can also be found in Gunnison. Call the Gunnison Country Chamber of Commerce at (970) 641–1501 for brochures and information about winter skiing, snowshoeing, and other outdoor activities. For further information about Waunita Hot Springs Ranch and the hours of operation, call (970) 641–1266.

Several snowshoeing or cross-country ski routes that range from easy to difficult are available in the area. The novice to intermediate route is the one to Waunita Pass. Up about 0.5 mile from Waunita Hot Springs Resort, follow the road on your left. The first several miles of this trail are along a private road. Please stay on the marked pathway. Climbing from 8,990 feet at the trailhead to an elevation of 9,200 feet, the trail again forks about 2 miles in.

The shortest and easiest route up to Waunita Pass at 10,300 feet is to stay to the left and continue up the old logging road that turns into Forest Road 763. This road winds its way through pockets of aspen and conifers, while paralleling Hot Springs Creek. The climb is gentle but constant, ideal for beginners looking for an easy route. All along the trail,

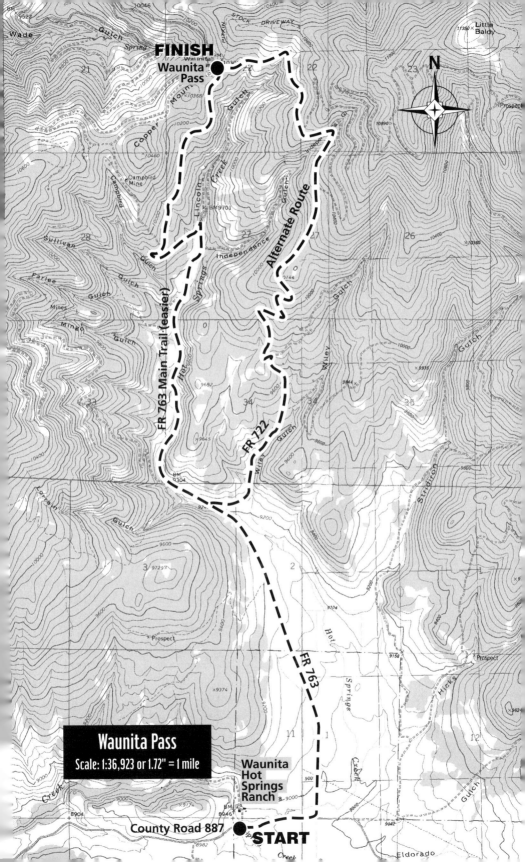

Directions at a glance

- The trail route begins at the Forest Service road closure. Go 0.5 mile east to the trailhead.

- Go left, heading north on the road. Stay on the road until it turns into Forest Road 763.

- Continue approximately 2 miles from the trailhead and look for a cutoff to Forest Road 722. The fork to the left continues up Forest Road 763. This is the easiest route.

- It's another 5.25 miles to Waunita Pass.

- Come back down the same way over the gentle downhill ski and snowshoeing path, or head east to Forest Road 722 for more challenging downhill back 4.6 miles until it intersects Forest Road 763.

- At this junction it's a short 2 miles back downhill to the trailhead.

Alternate route

- At approximately 2 miles from the trailhead, look for FR 722 sign. The trail will cut off to your right.

- Go right and enjoy a steeper climb that will meet Forest Road 763 back up at the top of Waunita Pass, approximately 4.6 miles from this junction.

- Forest Road 722 goes about 0.5 mile and then forks. Take left fork and continue to stay left.

- Forest Road 722 comes out at the top of Waunita Pass.

- Turn around and go back the same way for a more challenging route, or intersect Forest Road 763 at Waunita Pass and take the more gentle road back to the trailhead.

pockets of open water can be found along the creek in the early winter and early spring months. The warm water often disappears back into the ground but eventually comes out and feeds the hot springs back at Waunita Hot Springs Resort. It's about 1.75 miles up to Independence Gulch, and then another 0.5 mile to Lincoln Creek, where the trail does a hairpin switchback to the left. Then it's a 0.25-mile climb to Campbird Gulch, where the trail hairpins back to the right and continues climbing. From here, it's less than 1.5 miles to the top of the pass.

If you are looking for a more challenging route, take Forest Road 722 to the right at the fork, just over 2 miles from the trailhead. The route goes about 0.5 mile and then cuts back to the left. Keep following the road to your left, and you'll come to the top of Waunita Pass. The climb to the pass is steeper and narrower and is good for intermediate skiers and snowshoers. This trail parallels Wiley Gulch and provides an invigorating, but not too challenging, 4.6-mile route to the top of Waunita Pass.

Once you reach the top of Waunita Pass, you can loop back down by crossing over to either the novice or intermediate route back to the trailhead. Both roads are marked with wooden signs at the top of the pass.

Challenging glade skiing is available on the north side of Waunita Pass but is recommended for intermediate and advanced skiers only. It's easy to hike and ski down, but the trip back up is difficult.

Waunita Hot Springs Ranch is a very popular summer and winter destination. In the summer the hot springs are part of a busy dude ranch, and the pool is closed to day visitors. In the winter Waunita Hot Springs Ranch is a bed-and-breakfast, but the pool opens to the public if there are no groups staying there. It is also possible to walk in and get a room. If you are planning to swim or stay the night, they suggest you call ahead, just in case, to make sure their facilities are open. For $10 per person, it's an excellent idea to put a swimming suit in your car or daypack. The hot springs and pool facilities are a great way to unwind and relax tired muscles after a day in the backcountry.

How to get there

From Gunnison go approximately 16 miles east on U.S. Highway 50 to the Waunita Hot Springs turnoff at County Road 887. The turnoff will be on your left and is well marked. Go approximately 9 miles northeast to Waunita Hot Springs Ranch. Park along the roadside by the resort, but do not block the road or access area. The ski and snowshoe trail begins at the closed gate, but the official trailhead is approximately 0.5 mile past Waunita Hot Springs Ranch.

North Pole Hut

Uncompahgre National Forest, Ridgway, CO

Type of trail:	═══
Distance:	16 to 22 miles depending on snow conditions on the road.
Terrain:	The first miles follow flat and level roads, then moderately challenging climbs and descents all the way to the hut. The trail is long, often not well marked, and requires advanced navigation and map-reading skills.
Trail difficulty:	Intermediate; advanced navigation skills required.
Surface quality:	Ungroomed, but broken several times per week by skiers and snowshoers.
Elevation:	The trailhead is at 8,300 feet and the hut is at 10,000 feet.
Time:	5 to 7 hours in, 3 to 5 hours out.
Avalanche danger:	Low.
Food and facilities:	Because of the remoteness of North Pole Hut, winter users are advised to carry plenty of lightweight, high-energy snack foods, two liters of water, and emergency bivouac supplies, including a shovel, bivvy sacks or tarps, and no-cook food supplies. Grocery stores, hotels, and restaurant facilities can be found in the Ridgway area. If you plan to stay in Ridgway before your trip, call the Ridgway Area Chamber of Commerce at (800) 220–4959 or visit www.ridgwaycolorado.com. If you stay overnight in Ridgway, make sure you get up and plan for a very early start. Get on the trail by no later than 9:00 A.M. For more information about the hut system or guide services, contact the San Juan Hut System at (970) 626–3033, or visit www.sanjuanhuts.com.

The San Juan mountain range is the largest in Colorado and is a favorite for summertime mountaineers, rock climbers, mountain bikers, and hikers. In the wintertime it's a popular area for everyone from downhill and backcountry skiers to snowshoers and even ice climbers. The problem is that the San Juans are extremely steep and craggy, making them majestic in their beauty but difficult for backcountry skiers and snowshoers to access. The jagged ridges of the range tower far above treeline and offer very few skiable passes. Compounding this is the fact that the avalanche danger is often high.

In the mid-1980s Joe Ryan solved the problem of backcountry access for skiers in the San Juan Mountains by establishing his own hut system. He linked the 30-plus-mile stretch from Telluride to Ridgway with five

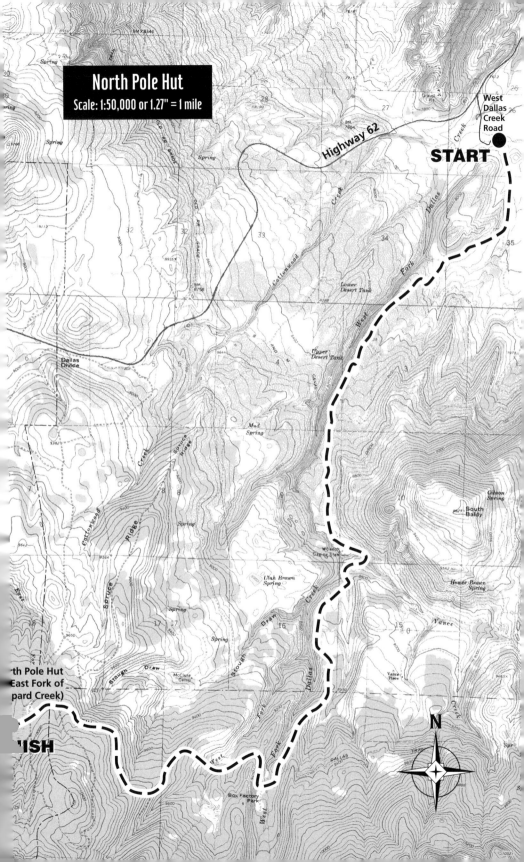

North Pole Hut

Scale: 1:50,000 or 1.27" = 1 mile

Highway 62

West
Dallas
Creek
Road

START

North Pole Hut
(East Fork of
pard Creek)

'ISH

N

huts, placing the structures along old logging roads and trails. The routes to and from the trailheads to the huts are designed for intermediate skiers, while the routes from hut to hut are more taxing and should be undertaken by more experienced and advanced skiers.

The North Pole Hut is remarkable for its remoteness, which may appeal to backcountry skiers who want to feel they're in the wild and view the surrounding mountain range the way it has looked for millions of years. Since the North Pole Hut is located just outside the border of the Mount Sneffels Wilderness Area, skiers will not hear any mechanized vehicles, just their own skis moving on the snow.

The North Pole Hut is located in a meadow on the East Fork of Leopard Creek. Generally there are no day skiers in the area. You have the trees and the mountains and the views of Hayden Peak and North Pole Peak to yourself. You can climb 12,987-foot Hayden Peak by its north ridge in almost any avalanche condition as long as you are careful to follow your tracks back down the north ridge. If fresh, deep powder is your love, and the avalanche danger is low, you can enjoy the ridges and slopes in the bowls around the hut. Or if you prefer an easier pace and mellow ski touring is what you love best, there are old roads and trails south of the hut.

Parties are advised to be under way on the trail no later than 9:00 A.M. It is likely that they will still be on the trail until nearly dark or possibly even after dark. The trail is not overly steep, but it is very long, and solid route-finding skills are necessary. A compass, topo map, and the ability to use them are a must. Everyone in the party should carry headlamps and flashlights with extra batteries. This trek to the North Pole Hut is going to require you to give great attention to the maps, compass, San Juan Hut System's instructions, tree blazes, metal flags, and signs. Unless you are able to handle the long trek and navigate extremely well in the woods, you may want to consider hiring a guide to lead you.

From the trailhead for the first 6.5 miles, follow the roads and very detailed instructions obtained from the San Juan Hut System until you intersect Dallas Trail 200. Head west on Dallas Trail into the national forest following very specific "blue-and-silver" diamond signs that are posted on the trees. The route along Dallas Trail is not well marked by the Forest Service, hence the numerous diamond signs and red flag markers!

The route along Dallas Trail goes up, down, and along the sides of hills to the west for approximately 4.2 miles through groves of conifers, aspen, and Gambel's oak. There are also open meadows, treeless hillsides, and always-spectacular views. The last 0.25 to 0.5 mile of the route to the hut is off the Dallas Trail. The hut is located north of the trail, in an open meadow west of some beaver ponds.

The current hut replaced the original yurt in 1995. It comes complete

Directions at a glance

- From the trailhead at West Dallas Creek Road, head south for approximately 6.5 miles. Begin no later than 9:00 A.M.

- Intersect Dallas Trail 200 and make a right, heading west. The road ends and the trail becomes narrow.

- Closely follow the blue-and-silver diamonds and red flag markers.

- Go west approximately 1 mile, and you'll intercept a wider road.

- Turn left, heading southwest, and follow the road for 0.5 mile.

- Look for trail signs and diamond markers. The road will continue southwest, but you'll make a right back onto Dallas Trail 200.

- Dallas Trail heads west, then northwest for 1.25 miles. Look for the wide jeep trail running north and south, intersecting Dallas Trail.

- Continue west on Dallas Trail 200 till it ends. Look for the meadow down below about 0.25 mile west.

- Drop down into the meadow to the west, and North Pole Hut lies across the meadow and about 0.1 mile up the hillside.

- To return, get an early start and follow the same route back to the trailhead and where you parked your vehicle.

with padded bunks that will sleep up to eight visitors. Other amenities include a propane cookstove, propane lamps, wood stove, firewood, axes, snow shovels, simple outdoor toilets, and all the necessary kitchen gear. Melting snow provides your water supply. Reservations are required, and the cost is $25 per person, per night. Representatives from the San Juan Hut System can be contacted by phone to discuss the route and update you on the latest snow conditions.

How to get there

From Montrose head south on U.S. Highway 550 approximately 25 miles to the town of Ridgway. Head toward Dallas Divide on Colorado Highway 62 for about 7 miles. Pass Forest Road 7 to Dallas Creek. At the next road, Forest Road 9, a sign reads WEST DALLAS CREEK. Turn left and go south on West Dallas Creek Road. The road passes through the Double RL Ranch. Depending on the time of year and road conditions, it may be possible to shuttle loads in 2 or 3 miles, drop them, and return your vehicle to the road head. You will want to check the snow forecast for the duration of your trip to make sure your car isn't snowed in.

Lizard Head Pass

Uncompahgre National Forest, Telluride, CO

Type of trail: ═══ ⬤

Also used by: Snowmobilers.

Distance: 5.5 miles to railroad trestle and back; 6.5 miles to the Hope Lake trailhead and back; 3.75 miles from the trailhead to railroad trestle, and then to end of trail along North Trout Lake Road (must leave shuttle vehicle); 7.5 miles from trailhead to railroad trestle, and then to end of trail along the North Trout Lake Road and return to trailhead.

Terrain: The trail follows an old railroad bed and is gradual and gentle for the first 2.75 miles. At the split, the trail to the right has moderate climbs to the end. The trail to the left continues on a road to the north end of Trout Lake.

Trail difficulty: Novice to intermediate.

Surface quality: Ungroomed, but usually well tracked by skiers and snowshoers.

Elevation: The trailhead at Lizard Head Pass is at 10,200 feet; the trail ends at 9,700 feet near outlet of Trout Lake.

Time: 3 to 5 hours.

Snowmobile use: Moderate.

Food and facilities: Facilities are sparse in the area, and gas, equipment, and groceries are best obtained before leaving Telluride. Lodging is best found in Telluride—where it is expensive—or back in Ridgway, where hotel and motel accommodations are much more reasonable. Call Telluride Visitor Service at (970) 728–3041, or visit www.tvs.org; or the Ridgway Area Chamber of Commerce at (970) 626–5181, or visit www.ridgway colorado.com. A few small towns can be found between Telluride and Lizard Head Pass, but most of these cater to summer visitors and are closed during the winter months. At the top of Lizard Head Pass, there are toilets provided by the Forest Service and the summit sign explaining the historical significance of the pass.

The trail begins at Lizard Head Pass and follows the old Denver & Rio Grande Railroad bed. The tracks have long since disappeared, but the railroad bed is still there and provides an easy-to-follow route from the pass back down through Lizard Head Meadows. From there the trail swings to the east and traverses the hill for about 1 mile. There are

Lizard Head Pass
Scale: 1:24,000 or 2.64" = 1 mile

good views to the north of Trout Lake as you ski or snowshoe in and out of timber stands. Continue along the trail until it reaches North Trout Lake Road. This area is popular with snowmobilers, so expect to find some noise and traffic.

The trail crosses over Lake Fork Creek, where there is an old railroad trestle. Although this is a scenic and somewhat historic view, the trestle is posted as unsafe and is chained off. Forest officials are very concerned that the weight of snow and people could collapse it. If you're a beginner, this is a good place to turn around and trek or ski back to the trailhead.

The trail splits after the Lake Fork crossing, and you're about 2.75 miles in from the Lizard Head Pass trailhead. The most scenic trip is 1.9 or 2 miles up Lake Fork Canyon, but here is where the trail turns from a novice to intermediate level. Go another 200 yards past the railroad trestle. You'll see a road heading uphill to the right. Ski another 1.5 miles to the Hope Lake trailhead bulletin board. Skiing or snowshoeing beyond this point is not recommended during winter months due to high avalanche danger about 0.25 mile down the trail.

The other trail at the Lake Fork crossing will head northwest (left), following North Trout Lake Road. After a fresh snow, it's a gentle downhill trek or glide for about 1 mile along the east side of Trout Lake. It's often plowed soon after a snowstorm, gets a lot of snowmobile use, and can be spotty. Follow North Trout Lake Road, which will bring you out

A winter picnic.

Directions at a glance

- From the trailhead at Lizard Head Pass, follow the old railroad bed east for 0.25 mile.

- The trail turns northeast for 0.5 mile and opens up above a large meadow.

- Continue on the trail that traverses the side of a hill for another 1.5 miles until reaching an old and unstable railroad trestle bridge. *Stay off the trestle—it is very unsafe.*

- Go 0.25 mile past the bridge and the trail will come to a T-shaped intersection.

- Intermediate and advanced skiers and snowshoers may want to take the trail to the right, heading up Forest Road 627 toward the Lake Hope trailhead.

- Beginners can turn around at the T-shaped intersection and ski the approximately 2.75 miles back to the trailhead.

- To continue at the intersection, beginners can make a left onto North Trout Lake Road. It's plowed and sometimes spotty, but it's a gentle glide all across the east side of Trout Lake.

- At the end of your ski or snowshoe tour, follow the same route back to the trailhead.

at the north end of the lake. Here the road connects back up to Colorado Highway 145. You can either reverse the trail at this point, or pick up that well-placed shuttle vehicle here at the Trout Lake junction.

During windy and stormy weather, Lizard Head Pass can be very uncomfortable. There are a few trees at the pass and trailhead area, but it's a lot of open hillside and meadows. The farther you go the fewer trees there are to serve as windbreaks and help block or break up the often cutting winds.

How to get there

From Telluride drive south on Colorado Highway 145 for 15 miles to Lizard Head Pass. Park on the side road to the east, or left, of the pass or on the turnout that's located several hundred yards north of the pass. Plowed parking is often difficult to find right after heavy snows.

Appendix

USDA Forest Service Offices

Rocky Mountain Regional Office
740 Sims
Lakewood, CO 80225
(303) 275–5350

Arapaho and Roosevelt National Forests

Supervisor's Office
240 West Prospect
Fort Collins, CO 80526
(970) 498–2769
www.fs.fed.us/r2/arnf

Boulder Ranger District
2140 Yarmouth Avenue
Boulder, CO 80301
(303) 541–2500

Canyon Lakes Ranger District
1311 South College
Fort Collins, CO 80524
(970) 498–1375

Clear Creek Ranger District
101 Chicago Creek
P.O. Box 3307
Idaho Springs, CO 80452
(303) 567–3000

Sulphur Ranger District
9 Ten Mile Drive
P.O. Box 10
Granby, CO 80446
(970) 887–4100

Grand Mesa, Uncompahgre, and Gunnison National Forests

Supervisor's Office
2250 Highway 50
Delta, CO 81416
(970) 874–6600
www.fs.fed.us/r2/gmug

Grand Valley Ranger District
2777 Crossroads Boulevard, Suite A
Grand Junction, CO 81506
(970) 242–8211

Gunnison Ranger District
216 North Colorado
Gunnison, CO 81230
(970) 641–0471

Norwood Ranger District
1150 Forest
P.O. Box 388
Norwood, CO 81423
(970) 327–4261

Medicine Bow-Routt National Forest

Supervisor's Office
2468 Jackson Street
Laramie, WY 82070
(307) 745–2300

Hahns Peak-Bears Ears
   Ranger District
925 Weiss Drive
Steamboat Springs, CO 80487
(970) 870–2284

Yampa Ranger District
P.O. Box 7
300 Roselawn Street
Yampa, CO 80483
(970) 683–4635

Pike and San Isabel National Forests

Supervisor's Office
1920 Valley Drive
P.O. Box 219
Pueblo, CO 81008
(719) 545–8737
www.fs.fed.us/r2/psicc

Leadville Ranger District
2015 North Poplar
Leadville, CO 80461
(719) 486–0752

South Platte Ranger District
19316 Goddard Ranch Court
Morrison, CO 80465
(303) 275–5610

San Juan National Forest

Supervisor's Office
15 Burnett Court
Durango, CO 81301
(970) 247–4874
www.fs.fed.us/r2/sanjuan

Columbine West Ranger District
110 West 11th
Durango, CO. 81301
(970) 884–2512

Pagosa Ranger District
180 Second Street
P.O. Box 310
Pagosa Springs, CO 81147
(970) 264–2268

White River National Forest

Supervisor's Office
900 Grand Avenue
P.O. Box 948
Glenwood Springs, CO 81602
(970) 945–2521
www.fs.fed.us/r2/whiteriver

Aspen Ranger District
806 West Hallam
Aspen, CO 81611
(970) 925–3445

Dillon Ranger District
680 River Parkway
P.O. Box 620
Silverthorne, CO 80498
(970) 468–5400

Holy Cross Ranger District
24747 U.S. Highway 24
P.O. Box 190
Minturn, CO 81645

Avalanche Information

Colorado Avalanche Information
   Center
geosurvey.state.co.us/avalanche

Avalanche Information Hotlines

Weather, snow, and avalanche
   information is updated daily on
   these hotlines.
Denver and Boulder, statewide,
   (303) 275–5360
Colorado Springs, statewide,
   (719) 520–0020
Fort Collins, northern mountains,
   (970) 482–0457
Summit County, (970) 668–0600
Aspen, (970) 920–1664
Crested Butte, (970) 641–7161
Durango, southern mountains,
   (970) 247–8187

Hut Reservations

Colorado Mountain Club-Boulder
 Chapter
825 South Broadway, Suite 40
Boulder, CO 80303
(303) 554–7688, (303) 441–2436
bcn.boulder.co.us/recreation/bcmc
Accepts reservations for the CMC
 cabin at Brainard Lake by CMC
 members only.

Elkton Cabins
P.O. Box 3128
Crested Butte, CO 81224
(970) 349–1815
Accepts reservations for three huts
 in Washington Gulch near
 Crested Butte.

Never Summer Nordic, Inc.
P.O. Box 1903
Fort Collins, CO 80522
(970) 482–9411
www.neversummernordic.com
Accepts reservations for all the
 Never Summer Nordic Huts.

San Juan Hut System
P.O. Box 773
Ridgway, CO 84432
(970) 626–3033
www.sanjuanhuts.com
Accepts reservations for all the San
 Juan Huts.

San Juan Snow Treks Ski Hut
 System
c/o San Juan Sports
111 Main Street
Creede, CO 81130
(719) 658–2359, (888) 658–0851
www.sanjuansnowtreks.com
Accepts reservations for the hut system near Creede, Colorado.

Tennessee Pass Cookhouse
(719) 486–1750, (719) 486–8114
www.tennesseepass.com

10th Mountain Division
 Hut Associaton
1280 Ute Avenue, Suite 21
Aspen, CO 81611
(970) 925–5775
www.huts.org
Accepts reservations for all of the
 10th Mountain Division Huts,
 Summit County Huts, Alfred
 Braun Huts, and the Friends Hut.

Guide Services

Aspen Alpine Guides, Inc.
P.O. Box 659
Aspen, CO 81612
(970) 925–6618
www.aspenalpine.com

Crested Butte Mountain Guides
P.O. Box 1061
Crested Butte, CO 81224
(970) 349–5430
www.crestedbutteguides.com

Paragon Guides
P.O. Box 130
Vail, CO 81658
(970) 926–5299, (877) 926–5299
www.paragonguides.com

Southwest Adventures
P.O. Box 3242
Durango, CO 81302
(970) 259–0370, (800) 642–5389
www.mtnguide.net

Chambers of Commerce

Aspen Resort Chamber Association,
 (970) 925–1940, www.aspen
 chamber.org

Breckenridge Resort Chamber, (970)
 453–6018, www.gobreck.com

Crested Butte Chamber of Commerce, (800) 545–4505, www.crestedbuttechamber.com

Estes Park Chamber Resort Association, (970) 586–4431, (800) 44–ESTES (37837), www.estesparkresort.com

Fort Collins Chamber of Commerce, (970) 482–3746, www.fcchamber.org

Glenwood Springs Chamber Resort Association, (970) 945–6589, www.glenwoodsprings.net

Granby Area Chamber of Commerce, (970) 887–2311, www.rkymtnhi.com

Grand Junction Chamber of Commerce, (970) 242–3214, www.gjchamber.org

Gunnison Country Chamber of Commerce, (970) 641–1501, www.gunnison-co.com

Idaho Springs Chamber of Commerce, (303) 567–4382, www.idahospringschamber.com

Leadville and Lake County Chamber of Commerce, (719) 486–3900, www.leadvilleusa.com

Nederland Area Chamber of Commerce, (303) 258–3936, www.nederlandchamber.org

Ouray Resort Chamber Association, (970) 325–4746, www.ouraycolorado.com

Ridgway Area Chamber of Commerce, (970) 626–5181, (800) 220–4959, www.ridgewaycolorado.com

Salida Chamber of Commerce, (719) 539–2068, (877) 772–5432, www.salidachamber.org

South Park Chamber of Commerce, (719) 836–3410, www.parkcham berofcommerce.org

Steamboat Springs Chamber Resort Association, (970) 879–0880, www.steamboat-chamber.com

Summit County Chamber of Commerce, (800) 530–3099, www.summitchamber.org

Telluride Visitor Services, (970) 728–3041, www.tvs.org

Vail Valley Chamber of Commerce, (970) 949–5189, www.vailvalleychamber.com

Winter Park Frasier Valley Chamber of Commerce, (970) 726–4118, www.winterpark-info.com

Nordic Centers

Ashcroft Ski Touring Center
312H AABC
Aspen, CO 80611
(970) 925–1971
www.pinecreekcookhouse.com
35 km of groomed trails

Aspen/Snowmass Nordic Trail System
c/o Ute Mountaineering
308 South Mill Street
Aspen, CO 81611
(970) 920–5120
www.utemoutaineer.com
60 km of groomed trails

Beaver Creek Nordic Center
Vail Resort
P.O. Box 7
Vail, CO 81658
(970) 845–5313
www.beavercreek.com
32 km of groomed trails

Beaver Meadows Resort Ranch
100 Marmot Drive, Unit 1
Red Feather Lakes, CO 80545
(970) 884–2450, (800) 462–5870
www.beavermeadows.com
40 km of groomed trails

Breckenridge Nordic Center
1200 Ski Hill Road
P.O. Box 1776
Breckenridge, CO 80424
(970) 453–6855
30 km of groomed trails

Cordillera Nordic Center
P.O. Box 988
Edwards, CO 81632
(970) 926–5100
12 km of groomed trails

Crested Butte Nordic Center
620 2nd Street
Crested Butte, CO 81224
(970) 349–1707
25 to 40 km of groomed track

Devil's Thumb Ranch
P.O. Box 750
Tabernash, CO 80478
(970) 726–8321
www.devilsthumbranch.com
105 km of groomed trails

Durango Mountain Resort
3001 West 3rd Avenue
Durango, CO 81301
(970) 247–9000 ext. 114, (970)
385–2114
www.durangomountainresort.com
16 km of groomed trails

Eldora Mountain Resort
P.O. Box 1697
Nederland, CO 80466
(303) 440–8700
45 km of groomed track

Frisco Nordic Center
P.O. Box 519
Frisco, CO 80443
(970) 668–0866
43 km of groomed trails

Grand Lake Touring Center
P.O. Box 590
Grand Lake, CO 80447
(970) 627–8008
www.grandlakecolorado.com/
touringcenter
35 km of groomed trails

Grand Mesa Nordic Council
P.O. Box 266
Cory, CO 81414
(970) 434–9753
outdoors.at/gmnc

Howellson Hill Ski Area
P.O. Box 775088
Steamboat Springs, CO 80477
(970) 879–8499
15 km of groomed trails

Keystone Cross Country Center
P.O. Box 38
Keystone, CO 80435
(970) 496–4275, (800) 427–8308
www.keystoneresort.com
26 km of groomed trails
50 km of ungroomed trails

Latigo Cross Country Ski Ranch
P.O. Box 237
Kremmling, CO 80459
(970) 724–9008, (800) 227–9655
www.latigotrails.com
65 km of groomed trails

Piney Creek Nordic Center
P.O. Box 223
Leadville, CO 80461
(719) 486–1750
www.tennesseepass.com
24 km of groomed trails

Snow Mountain Ranch YMCA of
   the Rockies
P.O. Box 169
Winter Park, CO 80482
(970) 726–4628, (970) 887–2152
www.ymcarockies.org
100 km of groomed trails

Solvista Golf & Ski Ranch
P.O. Box 1110
Granby, CO 80446
(970) 887–3384, (303) 629–1020,
   (800) 754–7458
www.solvista.com
40 km of groomed trails

Steamboat Springs Ski Touring
   Center
P.O. Box 775401
Steamboat Springs, CO 80477
(970) 879–8180
www.nordicski.net
30 km of groomed track

Sunlight Mountain Resort
10901 County Road 117
Glenwood Springs, CO 81601
(970) 945–7491, (800) 445–7931
www.sunlightmtn.com
29 km of groomed trails

Telluride Nordic Center
565 Mountain Village Boulevard
Telluride, CO 81435
(970) 728–6900, (866) 287–5016
www.telski.com
30 km of groomed trails

Ute Meadows Inn and Nordic
   Center
2880 County Road 3
Marble, CO 81623
(970) 963–5513
www.utemeadows.com
15 km of groomed trails

Vail Golf Course
458-X Vail Valley Drive
Vail, CO 81657
(970) 949–5750

Vista Verde Guest and Ski Ranch
P.O. Box 770465
Steamboat Springs, CO 80477
(970) 879–3858, (800) 526–7433
www.vistaverde.com
30 km of groomed trails

Resources

Backcountry Skiers Alliance
P.O. Box 3067
Eldorado Springs, CO 80025
(303) 494–5266
backcountryalliance.org

Colorado Cross Country Ski
   Association
P.O. Box 8937
Keystone, CO 80435
www.colorado-xc.org

Colorado Ski Country USA
1507 Blake Street
Denver, CO 80202
(303) 837–0793, (303) 831–SNOW
    (7669)
www.coloradoski.com

Cross Country Ski Areas
    Association
259 Bolton Road
Winchester, NH 03470
(603) 239–4341, (877) 779–2754
www.xcski.org

Winter Wildlands Alliance
910 Main Street, Suite 235
Boise ID 83702
(208) 336–4203
www.winterwildlands.org

About the Authors

TARI LIGHTBODY

A dedicated researcher and writer, Tari pens articles for local, regional, and national magazines, and has earned contributing credits for a host of national and international books. She has also written books in the romance, mystery, and intrigue lines.

Even while writing all of these books and articles, Tari is always "Mom" to her children—Daniel, Jeffrey, Matthew, and Jennifer.

ANDY LIGHTBODY

A lifelong outdoorsman, Andy loves to share his knowledge of the outdoors through articles, books, and broadcasts. His written works have been published by Petersen Publishing Company, Challenge Publications, *Consumer Guide,* and *Consumer Digest.* In addition, through broadcasts on CBS Radio, CNBC-TV, and FOX-TV, he has continued to report about myriad outdoor recreational opportunities and the importance of conserving the environment for today and for future generations.

Andy has served as a regional correspondent for *Fishing & Hunting News Magazine,* the host of the radio program *Colorado's Outdoor Minutes,* and is a regular contributor to many outdoor recreation magazines. Even while writing and broadcasting, Andy remains a dedicated "Dad."